Cooking My Way to Heaven

My Convent Life
&
Notre Dame Recipes

To Mary Lou,
God Bless you!

MARY ANN QUINN

Mary Ann Quinn

Scripture quotations in this book are from the New Revised Standard Version copyright © 1989, Division of Christian Education of the National Council of Churches of Christ in the United States of America.

Editing by Sister Mary Kathleen Glavich, SND

Photographs
Sister Myra Avsec, SND (cover)
Mary Ann Quinn (page 22)

Artwork
Cover, interior design, and art by Sister Mary Kathleen Glavich, SND

Icon on page 168 with the permission of Ruben M. Gallegos, Albuquerque, NM

ISBN-13: 978-1523815463
ISBN-10: 1523815469

Printed in the United States of America

DEDICATION

To the Sisters of Notre Dame of Cleveland, Ohio,
my religious family for many years,
and
to my mother, Dorothy Quinn, who allowed me
to follow my dream

CONTENTS

ACKNOWLEDGMENTS

Heartfelt thanks to the Sisters of Notre Dame of Chardon, Ohio, currently under the leadership of Sister Margaret Mary Gorman.

Endless thanks to the Sister cooks, all of whom have mentored me at one time or another. I am especially indebted to the group of Sisters who gathered with me to collect memories or shared them by phone. These include the following Sisters with their former names in parentheses: Sisters Veronica Blasko (Thaddea), who taught me so many culinary skills; Mary Ann Burke (Brigid), who provided many moments of humor; Jeanne Swindell (Lauramay); Theresa Gebura (Magdalae), who always promoted professional excellence; Janet Kondrat (Anthon); Julia Surtz (Emmet); Stefana Osredkar; Rita Marra; Ellenann Mach; Ann Patrick Mahon; and Mary Ann Cirino (Vincenta Marie).

These deceased cook Sisters too played an important role in my life: Sisters Myra Avsec (Antonmarie), who organized the meetings; Sister Marie Bernadette, Sisters Mary Dorotheus, Jordan, Eymard, Amata, Levina, Rosaire, and Trina, who cheered me on even in her last illness!

Thank you, too, to Sister Patricia Griesmer, who provided the recipe for Gruitze in Sister Dorotheus's handwriting on page 25.

Special thanks to Sister Sally Huston, who encouraged me to go ahead with an "idea" and preserve a piece of Notre Dame (ND) history.

I am extremely grateful and indebted to Sister Kathleen Glavich, SND, an accomplished author many times over, who polished my rough manuscript down to the last detail. As my mother would say, Thanks a million!

Thanks also to Karen Mansi, my housemate, who kept the household running by cleaning, cooking, doing laundry, and taking care of four cats! She also kindly listened to my writing and critiqued it as I went along.

Finally, I am grateful to Cora Martin, R.D., friend and colleague, who, besides advising and supervising my work as a Dietary Technician Registered, supported me in this writing venture.

INTRODUCTION

*As he went ashore, he saw a great crowd;
and he had compassion for them, because they
were like sheep without a shepherd; and he
began to teach them many things. When it
grew late, his disciples came to him and said,
"This is a deserted place, and the hour is now
very late; send them away so that they may go
into the surrounding country and villages and
buy something for themselves to eat." But he
answered them, "You give them something to
eat." They said to him, "Are we to go and buy
two hundred denarii worth of bread, and give
it to them to eat?" And he said to them, "How
many loaves have you? Go and see." When
they had found out, they said, "Five, and two
fish." Then he ordered them to get all the
people to sit down in groups on the green
grass. So they sat down in groups of hundreds
and of fifties. Taking the five loaves and the
two fish, he looked up to heaven, and blessed
and broke the loaves, and gave them to his
disciples to set before the people; and he
divided the two fish among them all. And all
ate and were filled; and they took up twelve
baskets full of broken pieces and of the fish.
Those who had eaten the loaves numbered
five thousand men.* (Mark 6:34–44)

When I was a young Sister by the name of Sister Sean
Maureen, this Scripture passage about Jesus feeding the

---

multitude touched my heart. Over the years, its meaning has continued to unfold and remains a subject of my meditation. Quantity foodservice, or "feeding a crowd," did in fact become my life's work, first inside the convent, then in school foodservice, and finally as a nutrition professional in long term care. One may think, "Not such a glorious profession." I can't help but recall my sister Bonnie exclaiming, "Cooking? You want to cook?!"

However, Jesus himself did foodservice. In the six Gospel accounts of the multiplication of loaves and fish, Jesus served not only with compassion but with generosity. There were leftovers! All were utterly amazed. Notice: Jesus first directed the disciples to do what they could. Then, he made up the difference. In my chosen profession, I too brought what I could of my own resources; and I know Jesus so often made up the difference!

Jesus prepared and served food other times. His first miracle was to provide wine at a wedding. After the resurrection, while some disciples were fishing, he cooked breakfast for them, grilling fish and bread on the shore. He added some of the fish they caught to the meal.

Then, too, Jesus chose to remain with us in a special meal, the Eucharist, or the breaking of the bread. At his last supper on the evening before Our Lord died, he gave us the Eucharist, an important meal where—as in all special meals—we share and celebrate. Jesus invites us to his table again and again until hopefully we all come together to feast at the eternal banquet of heaven!

A good cook can make such a difference with a meal. He or she not only has the opportunity to satisfy the hunger of others but the power to bring about joy, unity, and love in the process. I think of the movie *Babette's Feast.* In this story of a famous French chef, Babette, we learn that "to be a good cook is to be an artist who pours out her very self in love over and over and is never impoverished by the giving." The resemblance to our Lord's role in the Eucharist is striking.

After considering that Jesus fed the hungry and chose a meal as the setting for his expression of self-giving love, I think we can now conclude that the culinary profession is a notable one!

And so, for anyone who may enjoy a peek inside the cloister and a taste of convent cuisine, I offer this combination memoir/cookbook. Bon appetit!

PART I

<u>Memoir</u>

CHAPTER 1

THE BEGINNING

Let's start at the very beginning, a very good place to start! The hills were alive with *The Sound of Music* in the early sixties. Moviegoers everywhere made their way to theaters to meet the postulant Maria, who lived in a convent in the Austrian Alps. (A postulant is a person in the initial stage of becoming a woman or man religious.)

At the very time Maria was singing in the Alps, women were in fact entering convents in the U.S.A. in rather large numbers. I was one of those postulants, and my convent was on a Chardon hill in Geauga County, Ohio. There were many of us "Marias" then, complete with buster brown collar and black cape!

How did I arrive in Chardon? I was born on September 24, 1950, in Warren, a small town in northeastern Ohio. Patrick, Bonnie, and I were the children of Dorothy and Virden Quinn. I also have two brothers, Wiley and Gail, and a sister, Marianna, from my mother's previous marriage. Therefore I have numerous nieces and nephews.

Thanks to the generosity of my uncle Raymond Lonsway, I enjoyed the benefits of a Catholic education first at St. James Parish School and then for two years at John F. Kennedy High School in the Catholic Diocese of Youngstown. During those two years, I felt called to be a Sister of Notre Dame, so as a sixteen-year-old, I applied to the community. For my junior and senior years, I attended Notre Dame Academy in Chardon as an aspirant, or "prep," a girl who was preparing to be a Sister by living in the convent in "Prepville." In January 1969, my senior year, I became a postulant and moved up to the novitiate floor.

Mary Ann Quinn as an aspirant and
Bonnie, her sister, on a visiting Sunday

The Property

Sitting high on a hill and overlooking a small lake stood the Notre Dame Provincial Center, or Motherhouse, its impressive chapel facing Auburn Road. All around stretched the Sisters' farm, a "farmer's farm" with dairy cattle, Black Angus steer, and pigs. On every acre a seemingly endless variety of fruits and vegetables grew, and reigning supreme over all stood the apple orchard.

At the entrance gate, numerous apple trees along both sides of the road formed virtual fortress walls. I think the location of the orchard, presenting itself immediately at the convent gates, was appropriate. For if there is one food that conjures up endless memories for me of this convent on a hill, it would be the apple. A friend at work inquired once, "Did the nuns ever do anything with all those apples?" My answer: "Did they ever!"

Past the orchard, the road branched left and right, and there at the center of the divide stood the benevolent bronze figure of the Blessed Mother, a symbol of her place in the hearts of the Sisters here.

A Cook Sister

In that scenic home, I was destined to become a cook Sister. Cook Sisters, that's what we were, and that's how we were described by our co-Sisters in this teaching community. Cook Sisters desired to live religious life but did not want to do this as teachers. The cooks were "Apostles to the Apostles." This is what Sister Mary Christopher Rohner, director of junior professed Sisters (those under temporary vows), explained to me when I, a new cook Sister, was entrusted to her guidance. Cooks literally fortified the community for the front lines of education in the classroom.

In the early years of the Notre Dame Sisters of Cleveland, many young women came to the convent from large farm families, often of German descent. It so happened that some of these women were well versed in domestic arts, including the culinary arts, and became cook Sisters. And so, in the preparation of meals, German customs and food preferences were nicely provided for. Some young women simply preferred to serve within the community as cooks. Others were not entirely suited to pursue a degree in education but were very gifted and giving in other ways. These ministered within the community not only in foodservice but in health care, the business office, administration, household management and sewing, which included maintaining the traditional religious habit that all Sisters used to wear.

Instead of the black Notre Dame habit, cook Sisters wore a white habit as protection from the heat of the kitchen. This white habit was covered by a bright blue apron at work. Cook Sisters followed the same customs and prayed the same prayers as the other Sisters. However, often when the community was gathered for meals, prayers, and other activities, they were busy working in the kitchen.

Among the cooks there was notable camaraderie. Strong bonds of friendship were born out of their unique experience within the community of Notre Dame, bonds that still exist after so many years.

Foodservice is hard work, especially quantity foodservice. This was never more true than in my early days in the convent when cook Sisters worked seven days a week year round, except for an annual spiritual retreat of one week, or if you happened to get sick! I am proud to say that in the 80s I was on a committee that initiated change resulting in regular days off. Eventually vacation time was permitted for all Sisters, which

afforded necessary rest physically, mentally, and spiritually. As I recall our life as cook Sisters, rather than focusing on hardships (which really everyone experiences) I am inclined to identify with this line in a popular song of the 70s sung by Barbra Streisand, "The Way We Were": "It is the laughter we will remember whenever we remember the way we were."

CHAPTER 2

APPLES AND GRAPES

The Sisters knew the apple up close and personal because from the day they walked through the cloister doors, the apple greeted them morning, noon, and night! That's right. At every meal you could count on finding some form of apple served. I recall the aroma of cinnamon and apples wafting through the convent corridors. Even at end of day, walking through the dining room on the way to chapel, you would see those apples set out for an evening snack. Only the hale and hardy could eat one just before bed.

The Origin of Apples

Where does this noble fruit come from? Some research revealed that our apple, *Malus domesticus,* originated from the wild apple forests in the mountains of Central Asia. For example, in Kazakhstan outside the small village of Alma Ata (which translates "Father of the Apple") can be found blemish free apples growing in wild forests. Makes one want to visit this paradise!

Apples were in Europe and Asia hundreds of years before our European ancestors brought them to America. A folk story relates how John Chapman, aka Johnny Appleseed, would take seeds from the apple presses in eastern Pennsylvania and spread them over the western Appalachians and then on into the western plains. Who knows? Maybe one of Mr. Chapman's apple seeds begot one of the Sisters' orchard trees!

Today we know about the nutritional benefits of the apple. They are low in calories (about 50 calories per 100 grams), high in fiber, and rich in antioxidants, beta-carotene, and vitamin C. In those years, Sisters just knew they tasted good and it was probably true that an apple a day would keep the doctor away!

This noble fruit, the apple, was important to the culinary traditions of the Sisters, not solely for their nutritive value, but also because apples provided a source of income. Truly, one could say the apple paid for many a Sister's education. "How?" you may ask.

Large numbers of Sisters and an even larger numbers of apples combined to produce thousands of homemade pies that fed thousands of benefactors. That's how.

The annual September chicken barbeques featuring home baked apple pies should be answer enough for my friend who asked, "Did the nuns ever do anything with all those apples?"

In addition, they stored apples in big coolers, indexing them like books in a library by genus, size, color, baking, stewing, and eating, those to be used first, last, for cider, and so on. Apples were also pressed for juice, which was frozen and used year long at breakfast.

The Sisters' orchard by Notre Dame College and Regina High School that bordered on South Green Road no longer exists. But the orchard in Chardon is still visible from the road today and continues to provide income, health, and beauty all at once.

Grapes

The apple may have been important to the culinary traditions of the Sisters, but equally important was grape growing. Now there was a real monastic tradition! The Sisters kept this tradition and cared for vineyards on their Motherhouse and Notre Dame College properties.

Today we read about the nutritional benefits of grapes. They are rich in Vitamin C, polyphenols, antioxidants, and fiber. Back then, the Sisters just knew that they tasted really good and left stains on their white habits and hands to remember them by! Grapes served fresh in season and processed for juice and jelly were another source of nutrition year round.

OK. You are probably wondering…Did the Sisters make wine with so many grapes? Yes, they did, however, only after the inquisitive young women of the 60s arrived. They just had to try their hand at winemaking, first secretly in the maintenance supply room and then with full approval in the main kitchen. In the end wine was served to all—even rhubarb wine under the supervision of Sister Julia Surtz— and everyone was proud and VERY HAPPY!

The Origin of Vineyards

Charlemagne, sometimes described as "the Father of Europe," is credited with encouraging monasteries to plant vineyards, orchards, and herb gardens. He reasoned: The church needed a steady supply of altar wine. Planting vineyards would ensure a good supply, and quality could be carefully preserved. Monks, along with local villagers, provided the work force.

The vineyards of France soon became the vineyards of all of Europe. Monasteries thrived and provided education for laborers. As a result, Europe developed and flourished. This fact, I think, establishes the grape as a noble fruit right up there with the apple.

CHAPTER 3

GRUITZE

Historically pork has been central to German cuisine,
and German farmers in America found hogs economical
to raise on their very large farms. The same was true for
the religious community of Notre Dames, whose
heritage was German and whose customs, including
meal customs, reflected their roots. Pork meals were
plentiful, and there were a couple of especially favored
dishes. One was legendary: Gruitze!

When I was still new to the convent, one very early morning at breakfast I encountered an unfamiliar dish. I cast a perplexed look. A friend noticed and, trying to keep the monastic silence at table customary then, whispered, "It's delicious." The dish's aroma was pleasant, maybe sausage? The food scooped in the shape of six croquettes on a platter resembled thick oatmeal and appeared steamy hot. I took a portion, lifted my fork, and tasted "it." Instantly, I liked this dish, Gruitze.

Later that day I was told that the early German Sisters brought the recipe with them to America. You can imagine the surprise many years later when German Sisters who were visiting announced, "We know nothing of this Gruitze." During all the years that followed, the origins remained a mystery—that is, until my curiosity had to be satisfied and I started poking around.

From an old school text, *The New Nation. American Popular Culture Through History* by Anita Vickers, I learned that pioneer German immigrants were famous for introducing one-pot meals, often incorporating pork, broth, and cereal or grains. Two examples are German Panhasse and Philadelphia Scrapple. Getting close!

Further research revealed that, depending on local availability, substitute grains were used. In place of buckwheat for Panhasse and steel-cut oats for Philadelphia Scrapple, barley or rice might be used. These two grains were available in the West and South regions of the U.S.A. Hmmm. Interesting.

A few years passed. Then I googled Gruitze and finally struck gold! Matthew Rowley, a food writer, told on his blog, "Rowley's Whiskey Forge," about his search for his great grandmother's recipe for a similar breakfast dish. He found a recipe for Gritz credited to

Mrs. W.G. Bohnsack in a book titled *Kinderheim
Kookbook* published in 1927 in Addison, Illinois. There
it was, so closely resembling Notre Dame Gruitze! The
author unfolded the mystery all at once by linking
German roots, name, and recipe. He further explained
that a dish called Goetta, a popular German porridge,
was found in southern Ohio near Cincinnati and around
Covington, Kentucky. This discovery was all the more
exciting, knowing that the Notre Dame Sisters arrived
and settled in Cleveland, Ohio, and Covington,
Kentucky, following their German countrymen and
women. Mr. Rowley stated, "Its name is a transliteration
into English of the Plattdeutsch (Low German) word
götta, meaning groats (i.e., hulled cracked grains). In
standard High German, the word is Grütze, a cognate of
our own Southern grits." Goetta strikingly resembled his
dish and mine.

There we have it. Mystery solved. It is very likely
that barley was substituted for wheat in the Covington
area, considering that many distilleries were located in
the region, and we know what grain they used!

Finally, you may wonder with such strange names as
Scrapple and Grits what kind of pork was used. I assure
you the Sisters used pork shoulder, butt, and hocks.
Customary in Europe, however, was the use of other
pork parts, including head meat. I'm not sure why our
German guest Sisters did not recognize ND Gruitze.
That remains a question. Perhaps variation of cuisine
within Germany was the reason.

One morning in the 60s I encountered Gruitze. Forty
years later, I discovered its origins. Gruitze: A German
recipe and a Notre Dame tradition.

Dear Sr. Mary & Patricia,

Gruitze

Boil a piece of pork about a lb.
or less covered with water until
tender, grind or chop with a small
piece of onion, a pinch of sage or
thyme - optional. Add to the liquid
that the pork was cooked in should
be about 2 qts. Add 1/2 bag of
pearl barley. Salt & pepper to
taste.

Bake about 2 to 2 1/2 hrs. until
barley is finished at 300°.

If there this is not enough
broth add a little water.

God bless you - God heals.

Sr. Mary D. Rothius SND

CHAPTER 4

THE BROWN MEAL

Meal planning guidelines suggest a balance of color, texture, and flavors to promote appeal and enhance appetite. Some of this was seemingly thrown out the window when Sisters put together "The Brown Meal," a description used endearingly by the Sisters. Remarkably, this meal was so favored that it was served regularly at noon on Saturdays, when most Sisters were home from school.

No trouble with appeal here! The fragrance of sage seasoned pork croquettes baked with toasted bread-crumb crust captured one's attention right away. Added to this was savory sauerkraut seasoned with caraway, bacon drippings, and brown sugar. Served alongside were real mashed white potatoes with brown gravy. A side of fresh cinnamon applesauce and a dessert of homemade bread pudding, and The Brown Meal was complete!

While pork was preferred, beef dishes were enjoyed as well. It took me many years to discover that "convent hamburgers" were actually based on a German recipe and greatly resembled what is characteristic of meat loaf.

I recall, more than once, friends seeing that I was about to prepare hamburgers, begging me not to put "all that other stuff" in the ground meat. They wanted their all-American burger of ground round or sirloin unadulterated. I complied, despite being taught to add breadcrumbs; egg; ground fresh herbs, such as parsley, onion, and celery; a little milk; and other spices, including ketchup and mustard. Also added was ground cooked meat left over from previous meals that had entrées of beef roast or pork roast. The leftover meat was ground in the Griswald meat grinder through small holes and seasoned as desired. Added to the fresh ground meat, it acted as a binder and filler in the same way that breadcrumbs or rice does for meat loaf, stuffed peppers, and the like.

Two other beef meals traced to German cuisine were meat pinwheels served with hot apple-raisin sauce or gravy, and meat dressing. These were less popular with the young Sisters but well liked by the older Sisters. For pinwheels, ground cooked meat, sometimes with cheese added, was spread over a rectangle of biscuit dough. The rectangle was rolled up tightly, making a log. This log was sliced into pinwheels, which were baked.

Sister Dorotheus, who was in charge of our kitchen, started talking about serving meat dressing soon after the holidays. No doubt since she came from a large German family, she was familiar with this dish. Essentially meat dressing is stuffing as we know it, except with the addition of meat gleaned from cooking a carcass for soup.

Now may be a good time to mention that the Sisters of Notre Dame lived the vow of poverty in very real ways. In the culinary department, this was illustrated by the creative use of leftovers. By the way, leftovers are incorporated in many favorite food dishes. Italians add them to ravioli, Middle Eastern groups to stuffed grape leaves, and our European ancestors to stuffed cabbage. Everyone uses leftovers in homemade soups!

Kitchen Tools

The Griswold Food Grinder was likely a precursor to the current day Cusinart. This versatile tool was commonly found in households of the late 1800s and early 1900s, along with other cast iron cookware: fry pans, stew pots, roasters, and cake molds, such as the mold for the lamb cake that graced the Easter table.

Also found in the convent kitchen was the cast aluminum food chopper. This was a well-used tool in the Motherhouse kitchen. (Very important at apple pie time!) Leftover pork or beef roast was often chopped, thus speeding up the otherwise lengthy time required to prepare a large quantity of food for a meal.

All the meals were very substantial. Providentially, a good metabolic rate that comes with youth, along with generous doses of housework and gardening, kept most of us thin. Housework, mind you, was often scrubbing and waxing the convent floors (including the large chapel) as well as the floors of schools that the Sisters ran. Gardening was tending to the truck farm and orchards. One exception to the Sisters' workload was the dairy farm.

BOOK
BAG
OVAL
BOX
FOLD
BOOT
COR

NO
PANCAKE
parsol

P
Purse
Butter
Coprcor

SNE
PILT

Pd
N

SI

T
9

CHAPTER 5

THE DAIRY FARM

From the front of chapel, gazing above the apple and pine treetops and across Auburn Road, one could see the dairy farm, carefully tended by the Sisters' farmers, Harold and Steve.

Steve oversaw most chores and shared tasks with Harold, who took care of the pigs. (We could always tell when Harold had been in the elevator.) Between the two men, a regular supply of fresh milk was delivered to the kitchen every day or so. On some days, milk was more abundant than others, depending on the time of year, weather, and so forth. At times, as many as fourteen five-gallon milk cans arrived!

Steve was a sturdy man of middle age, polite, quiet, and shy. On days when Harold, the usual milkman, was off work, Steve came to the kitchen very early in the morning, just after Mass and before breakfast. He arrived with a wooden dolly of milk cans. To the Sisters' "Good morning, Steve," he just smiled back his greeting. Then he went about the task of stacking milk cans two high, side by side in the milk cooler.

Next, he checked the apple cooler for containers holding scraps for the hogs, such as apple and vegetable peelings. He loaded these onto his long, empty milk dolly and then waited quietly off to the side for his breakfast tray. When it was ready, Steve left with his dolly and breakfast and took the elevator down to the workmen's dining room, which was on the first floor.

Harold was a short, slight, middle-aged man, scraggly in appearance. He usually wore a smile on his bristle-bearded face. On his head was a cap, tilted back enough to reveal his face. One could not help notice a nervous twitch that made his eyes squint, cheeks wrinkle, and his head move with a little jerk. Once in a while, his face bore a hint of sadness. A crippled leg caused Harold to limp, and his crippled arm forced him to carry items mostly with his right hand assisted by the wounded limb. Still, he managed to swing those five-gallon cans around with enough strength and control to get the job done!

Harold knew his job well and was very dependable, showing up no matter what the weather. Working as a farmer at the convent, I suspect, was probably all that his limitations allowed. Interacting with the Sisters seemed to bring him joy. Harold loved working for the Sisters, and the Sisters loved Harold!

In contrast to Steve, Harold was loud, especially in his spontaneous, booming laughter. Never mind convent silence! One morning, newly assigned to manage the dairy cooler, I was to receive the milk and prepare breakfast for Harold. Always polite, Harold bellowed, "Mornin', Sister!" I replied, "Mornin', Harold!" (with a "back at ya" tone in my voice). He grinned at my retort and laughed aloud. The next day, same thing. This time he added, "How are you today, Sister?" I replied, "Peachy!" Harold roared, "Peachy? Peachy? Ha, ha!" Sister Mary Dorotheus, the head cook, looked our way.

The following day, when Harold arrived, he immediately called out, "MORNIN', PEACHY! HA, HA, HA." The glare across the kitchen from Sister Dorotheus was signal that I had some explaining to do.

Everyone else, including me, could not help but laugh at Harold's utter enjoyment. He eventually toned it down when I hinted that he was disturbing the peace. Nevertheless, ever after, he greeted me, "Mornin', Peachy!"

This simple fellow served the Sisters faithfully for many years. Eventually the dairy farm closed and milk was purchased. Any Sister remembering those farm days surely remembers Harold, with a smile and a laugh.

Buttermilk Soup

"A thunderstorm is expected tonight," Sister Dorotheus informed me, "so take out a can of milk with cream on top and set it at the end of the pot and pan shelving to remain at room temperature. The thunderstorm will speed up the curdling process."

Sister's goal was Buttermilk Soup for the whole house at the end of the week. Indeed, she was right; the thunderstorm did cause the milk to curdle. Sister grew up on a farm herself and had a wealth of knowledge about such things. As for culinary skills, she excelled there too, a truth I soon discovered.

Buttermilk Soup was a treat for most of the community and an acquired taste for some of us. Not for everyone, this cold soup with characteristic sour bite! It could very well be described "a culture shock," in both the ethnic and scientific understanding of the word *culture*!

What helped make this dish more palatable was the customary addition of sweet chunks of cake or cookies as croutons. Slices of fresh peaches, pears, or other summer fruit were sometimes complements to the cold buttermilk.

My first experience of this German delicacy occurred as a novice at a silent noon meal. That's right, no talking! (At the time, the community observed the monastic custom of silent meals when all listened to a spiritual book read aloud.) Unfortunately, I was not having any lofty spiritual thoughts as I tried to consume the cold treat before me. Obedience and the good manners my mother instilled in me won the day. Though I never developed a great liking for it, I did eventually manage to appreciate a well-prepared Buttermilk Soup.

Once the dairy farm was discontinued, Buttermilk Soup disappeared. Sister Dorotheus explained, "You will never derive the same flavor from homogenized milk because the flavor results from fresh cow's milk, or "raw" milk. Thickening occurs by natural fermentation of bacteria only present in fresh cow's milk, and these bacteria give buttermilk its unique flavor. Homogenization destroys this particular flora."

Thick Milk

German farmers referred to "dicke milch" (thick milk). Patricia B. Mitchell, author of the pamphlet "German Cooking in American," quotes a source as saying, " 'Dicke milch' was part of our summer food fare in East Germany, close to the Polish border." This discovery touched me since my German roots come from the same geographic area. Should I perhaps be positively genetically disposed to this summer recipe?

Incidentally, yogurt is a similar by-product of milk that is allowed to ferment with specific bacteria targeted for flavor.

Other Dairy Fare

Milking cows provided the Sisters with some dairy rich foods. Besides buttermilk, we had fresh milk to drink and fresh cream for coffee and whipping. Several convent favorites were dairy-based. For example, the breakfast menu was often cheese slices served with bread and jelly or baked egg custard cut in square portions. Let's not forget French toast made with real French bread, soaked the night before in egg custard and then fried on the grill the next morning.

Cottage cheese was served as dinner entrée with a baked sweet potato and a hot vegetable. Other meatless entrées frequently prepared for Lent or Friday suppers were Savory Cheese Casserole, a dish related to breakfast custard, and sweet rice with cheese slices.

A Friday specialty was Swedish eggs. This dish was prepared by creating little nests of shredded cheese. A cracked egg was dropped into the center of each nest. Then milk was dribbled around each one to moisten the cheese. After baking, the individual portions were arranged on platters.

Homemade pudding made of whole milk, fresh eggs, and a cornstarch mixture was a regular dessert.

The Sisters enjoyed what every farm family enjoys: a wonderful variety of dairy-based foods that were comforting, nourishing, and excellent sources of Vitamin D, calcium, and phosphorous.

CHAPTER 6

"DIRECT CONTACT" IN A KITCHEN

Sister Mary Dorotheus, affectionately called "Dorothy dear," was in her late 60s, tall, with frameless convent eyeglasses that we novices called CGs. She usually appeared jolly, but her smile sometimes came along with a correction or admonition. After all, her job was to ensure good meals for all the Sisters and a few workmen. She was gifted in her ability to plan meals and organize everything and everyone. Hers was a huge task, especially because she personally trained each of the younger cooks, including me.

A few years ago, not having seen Sister for quite awhile and hearing that at the amazing age of 101 she was declining, I visited her. Recognizing me, she exclaimed with a teasing grin, laughing eyes, and a chuckle, "Have you had any direct contact lately?" I instantly recalled an old lesson learned years before. I will share this, but first, you must tour the kitchen.

The Notre Dame Kitchen

When I arrived at the Chardon Motherhouse, there were about eight Sisters who prepared meals for between 300 and 400 Sisters. In the summer, that number increased to close to 600 because all Sisters returned there when schools closed for vacation. Most Sisters were involved in schools at that time.

Almost everything was prepared from scratch back then. We "put up" the fruits and vegetables from the farm, canning and freezing these for use year round. Black Angus cattle and hogs were raised for butchering and provided meat. Cows were our source of dairy products. Naturally the convent kitchen area was enormous.

On the first floor was a delivery area with a wide, automatic entrance door and several big carts for transporting food. Here, too, were a large storeroom and two walk-in freezers.

The kitchen, located on the second floor, had several classic, individual walk-in coolers, complete with solid wood doors. It was designed with an island range, including open flame gas burners and hot plate areas, convenient for sliding large kettles of soup from back to front. Below were three standard gas ovens.

In later years a large stainless steel, rectangular tilt fry-stew pan was added. The lid could be up or down, depending on its use. This unit was very versatile in that one could fry pancakes at breakfast, prepare soup for lunch, and make spaghetti and meatballs in it for supper.

On the other side of the island range was a large griddle, a four-burner stove top with oven below, and a large fryer. Off to one side of the island was Sister Dorotheus's office. Bordering this were cupboards, stainless steel tables, and racks of pots and pans. Beyond the main kitchen and adjoining the professed Sisters' dining room was a scullery (a room for dishing out food and doing dishes).

Meals prepared in this big kitchen were sent off on carts to the adjoining dining room, three other dining rooms, and the infirmary.

35

The kitchen's main open space was a high traffic area. It had an entrance from a hall that led to chapel one way and to convent rooms in the other direction. Next to the entrance, a shiny tile wall went up to within two feet of the ceiling. Besides providing air, this short wall allowed kitchen noise to filter out and a few potholders from occasional friendly warfare to fly out.

Just inside the entrance was the infamous butcher block, where we all learned our meat cuts, often under the tutelage of Sister Thaddea, an expert in all things meat related. Opposite the block was the walk-in meat cooler, complete with meat hooks to hang hams and the like.

On the left of the open area was another room with spice racks on the right, the bread table, which was a large wooden cutting board (where all of our donated Hough Bakery loaves were cut). Farther back were the vegetable/apple cooler, the vegetable preparation area and the walk-in bread and bakery cooler.

Finally, there was the back room. Here were table and chairs and a two-compartment sink provided for work. After hours, the room was a "cook hang-out" for conversation, a card game, or other recreational activity.

Learning the Ropes

Now picture the huge kitchen with Sisters busy at work in every location, seven days a week, all year. You can imagine with such a large community to feed there was much work to be done and lots for a new novice to learn. Yes, after six months of being a postulant, I donned a habit with a white veil and began the next stage of formation: a two-year novitiate.

Sister Sean Maureen as a Notre Dame novice

I was anxious to learn, so much so that I tended to move about hurriedly. One day, I was racing from place to place so I could finish on time for Evening Prayer. Sister Dorotheus, a tall figure in a white habit, jumped in front of me, forcing me to stop dead in my tracks. Smiling she said, "Slow down! You won't get done any faster by rushing so!" I was embarrassed then; however, her words proved true in time.

As a Sister in my twenties, I thought I knew some things too, when in fact I had barely begun to learn. Is it not a characteristic of youth seeking independence to sometimes fail to appreciate the wisdom of others? But mentors can prevent a few stumbles.

Not long after the racing incident, Sister was making a big pot of soup. I noticed that in her effort to taste test it, she dropped her spoon to the floor. Much to my horror she picked up the spoon from the floor and inserted it directly into the boiling soup.

"Aha! I will let her know that was not sanitary!" I thought. And so I spoke up. "Sister Dorotheus! That spoon had direct contact with the floor and you picked it up and put it in the soup. That spoon was full of germs!" Amazing that we all survived our mothers' kitchens, when one stops to think about it!

Sister laughed at my outrage and said, "Sister, do you think any germ on the spoon could survive the boiling broth?" She was right, I had to admit. Boiling at 212° would take care of the problem!

My shock and disbelief quickly dissolved with the truth of her words. Sister never forgot that scene involving direct contact with the floor and neither did I. It remained a point of connection whenever we met over the years.

Truth be told, a couple years later, another Sister while removing a large, heavy pan of meat loaf from the oven, burned her hand, and then lost her grip on the pan, spilling its contents on the floor. I helped her scoop up the meat and clean the floor quickly before anyone else appeared! Back in the oven the meat loaf went for a few minutes before being served for dinner. OK! What would you have done with 150 Sisters expecting their dinner in ten minutes? If it is any consolation, the convent was always super clean! Novices swept and mopped the kitchen floor every day. Sister Dorotheus, I forgot to share this event with you!

I will always consider it a good thing that I had "direct contact" with Sister Dorotheus.

CHAPTER 7

POTATO HOUSEWORK

Each area of meal preparation (meat, potato, dairy, soup, vegetable, bread, and desserts) was referred to as "housework." Rotation occurred regularly, and thus an apprentice like me learned each area. I worked under the direction of a more experienced cook assigned to that area and always with oversight from Sister Dorotheus.

"Milk housework" for the day meant receiving fresh cans in the morning and working in the milk cooler. It also entailed washing and sanitizing the cans and then stacking them upside down to dry overnight for Harold to pick up in the morning.

"Potato housework" was combined with dairy duties. I learned to prepare potatoes in more ways than I could ever have imagined: mashed, pan-fried, oven fried, deep fried, roasted, baked, boiled, cubed, sliced, halved, crumbed, patties, cold salad, hot German, escalloped, au gratin, creamed, dilled, with parsley, with paprika, and so on.

A potato peeling machine was operated by a group of novices most mornings. If they didn't pay attention, the machine ran too long and produced marble-sized potatoes. Afterwards, the novices delivered the freshly peeled potatoes to the kitchen, where cold water was added to prevent the potatoes from turning brown. The large pots of potatoes were then stored in the milk cooler. The rest was up to me!

I became skilled in slicing and cubing really fast, using a technique that involved holding the potato in the left hand and cutting it into shapes with the knife in the right hand, never losing grip on the potato until depositing the shapes into another pot. Nifty, I thought!

Besides being able to be prepared in numerous appetizing ways, potatoes are also economical, easy to grow, and can be stored for long periods of time under stable conditions. Potato patties, with origins from northern Germany, were particular favorites of the Sisters. The key ingredient of this recipe is nutmeg, often used to flavor various dishes in northern Germany. It is a spice favored by their Scandinavian neighbors. Potato patties were often prepared from leftover mashed potatoes or any potato that could be ground, seasoned, and then formed and grilled.

The Sisters did not grow their own potatoes but purchased them from a farmer. He kept a supply for the Sisters in a dark cellar below one of the country homes on the Motherhouse property. This cottage was used now and then for visitors or retreats, but was often left quietly unused. Periodically, Sisters would drive to this location to pick up a hundred pounds or so of potatoes from the storage cellar.

I went along once on this task with a Sister who was training me. The cellar entrance was one of those old-fashioned, slanted wooden door entrances, typical of coal cellars familiar to me from my childhood. The two wooden doors slanted away from the side of the house and opened upwards. One entered by stepping down into the dark cellar. Neither my companion nor I was anxious to go inside this dark unknown. However, she bravely proceeded to venture into the cellar ahead of me.

Next followed a scene like the one in the movie *E.T.* where the children first encounter their extraterrestrial guest. One child screams at the sight of E.T., and then E.T screams back. This invites another scream from the child. Screams go back and forth for a minute. Sister saw tall, skinny white figures in the darkness. She screamed, and then I screamed at her scream. You get the picture! What were the white streaks? Nothing more than the eyes of potatoes that had been in storage for a very long time, growing straight up in the darkness, straining toward a faint beam of light. That was the last time Sister or I went to the potato cellar!

The Origin of Potatoes

The popularity of potatoes is another indication of German heritage! Potatoes were introduced to Germany by Frederick the Great (1712–1786). He ordered the planting of potato seeds, even posting soldiers in fields to encourage farmers. The towns-people of Kolberg protested: "The things have neither smell nor taste, not even the dogs will eat them, so what use are they to us?" Today visitors to Frederick's palace place a potato on his tomb slab.

Potatoes are thought to have originated in Peru, where they are still found in rich variety. A friend, a native of Peru, confirms this and is fond of the little purple ones. It is believed the Spanish conquistadors in Peru brought potatoes to Spain and subsequently to all of Europe. That would include Ireland!

CHAPTER 8

BREAD, BAKERY, AND ALL THINGS SWEET

Friends who have traveled to Germany tell me that bread is part of every meal, and hearty bread at that, like rye and pumpernickel. For almost every breakfast in the convent, bread and cheese with jelly or jam accompanied by fresh fruit or juice was served. Bread and cheese for breakfast was foreign to me. Cornflakes and shredded wheat were our fare at home. Now, many years later, this German custom is one I have adopted and continue to enjoy right here in the U.S.A.

In keeping with the traditional German routine at noontime, a large dinner type meal was served, including a plate of sliced bread. The evening meal was a lighter fare, often sandwiches or a casserole. In addition, the Sisters had a midmorning and midafternoon snack and, if they wished, a night snack, all featuring bread. In keeping with convent poverty, a plate of "end bread" was placed on the table at each main meal. These small pieces were used to sop up every bit of the meal, leaving clean plates.

For me, the variety of breads the convent offered was a new experience. I remember my first sight of a round loaf. I was curious about the slices of bread on the serving plate that were shaped like a heel or a filled-in horseshoe. A trip to the kitchen solved that mystery as I observed a Sister cook at the bread table slicing bread. There it was! She picked up a round loaf, cut it in half, and then laid it down on its fresh cut side. Sister began cutting neat slices, from small at the ends to large at the center. This was very different from sliced bread on the store shelves. And much more delicious, I might add! The abundance of bread and other bakery was due to frequent donations by a local Cleveland bakery, the famous Hough Bakery, no longer in existence.

Hough Stuff

For many years the Sisters benefited from overage bakery at the Hough headquarters. Not only was a great assortment of whole bread loaves, sliced bread, and rolls donated, but many other delectable sweet treats as well. There were pies, cakes, pastries, sweet rolls, fruit and custard Danishes, and cookies (especially those cookies with the big chocolate dollop in the center). I see these nowadays advertised as "Chinese Cookies."

The pies were plentiful in summertime and at holidays. Who can forget Hough pumpkin and mincemeat pies? There also were fruit, cream, and custard pies. They sometimes got a bit smashed but tasted the same! Donations occurred all year, but especially in the summer, when it was hot and humid, a condition under which fresh bakery does not hold well. We had to be especially careful of custard bakery, as these items were not artificial but real baked egg custard. Frequently custard items were tossed and discarded for safety unless we were assured of their freshness.

Cakes were just beautiful! Rich, layered, and tastefully frosted they came, including little hats with thick icing after Mother's Day. Many cakes lost some beauty in transport, but we loved them just the same. And Danishes! I can still see in my mind's eye and recall the exquisite taste of the cheese Danishes, some small, some large, even cake size! When they appeared at breakfast, you knew you would be treated to a great experience of flavor and a satisfaction that stayed with you throughout the morning.

How did these bakery donations get processed? A telephone call came from the bakery, and then a convent workman was dispatched with a truck loaded with cardboard banana boxes and pie racks. When he arrived, he had to pick up specific items by a certain time. If not, someone else would be called, or worse, all goodies would be thrown out! The bakery had fresh products in the oven. They needed the shelves.

Back at the convent, cooks and novices were informed and ready to receive the donated bakery. With calls coming later in the day, this meant the truck would arrive late, perhaps even after dinner. As many as a dozen Sisters worked to sort, wrap, and package the bakery for the cooler or freezer until the last crumbs were swept and the lights were turned off, however long it took.

The late evening work was a small price to pay for such treats and a regular supply of hearty breads. There were dry spells when our supply of bread would get very low. The Sisters placed a statue of St. Joseph in the window with his back to the kitchen, and sure enough, St. Joseph, the Provider, saw to it that we received bread not long after. Then, the statue was turned face forward to grace the kitchen window! Another German tradition, I suspect. All through my years of religious formation, the Sisters had bakery bread unlike any I have had since!

45

When we did not receive bakery donations, we baked our own sweet treats. Special feast days or holy days in the church calendar were celebrated by a sweet roll at breakfast or a dinner roll with the main meal of the day. Cakes or cookies made an appearance then too.

There seemed to be a lot of refrigerator dough cookies, something new to me, for we seldom had such treats at home. I took a shine to these and the interesting process of making the dough ahead of time, shaping it into rolls or pinwheels and wrapping it in wax paper to be stored in the cooler. How convenient it was to pull these out to bake when they were needed! We then sliced the dough to form cookies, placed them on cookie sheets, and baked them for a sweet treat. My personal favorites were butterscotch cookies and pinwheel cookies made with date filling.

Easter Treats

The week before Easter the convent workmen pulled the large truck into the delivery entrance. It carried an abundance of hot cross buns from Hough Bakery's central store. During Lent the bakery featured this Christian sweet roll because Cleveland, Ohio, was then and still is a melting pot of Eastern European immigrants. These folks have a great appetite for hot cross buns and other ethnic and holiday baked goods.

The week after Easter yet another sweet load of Hough bakery including lamb cakes arrived. The lamb stands for Jesus, the lamb of God, who died and rose to save us. In those years the lamb cake was presented in a windowed cake box, making it look like a wonderful gift and it surely was that! The customer took that gift home to the family Easter table where I am certain all little children seeing it could hardly wait to sample a slice. Wait a minute! Not just the children, but *everyone* looked forward to this dessert. I know the Sisters did. The leftover cakes that came in that day were well received. Some of them looked pretty much intact. The culinary representations of the Paschal Lamb, reminded us of Christ's love and added to our Easter celebration.

Fittingly, Sister Mary Dorotheus baked her own lamb cakes and presented these to benefactors as an Easter gift from the Sisters. Those of us who worked in the kitchen can surely recall how she plowed through making a couple dozen cakes. (We washed her dishes and cleaned up after her!) In the end, near perfect lamb cakes were delivered, cellophane wrapped, to friends. Dare I say it? Even nicer than Hough's!

CHAPTER 9

THE WAY WE WERE

As new cooks learned each aspect of quantity food preparation from an experienced cook, we learned by our mistakes as well. This was truer for some more so than others, or so it seemed for Sister Mary Brigid, a very Irish Sister with sparkling blue eyes, freckles, and a spirited manner.

Back then, it was a daily custom in religious life to ask pardon for errors and request a penance before the novice directress and other novices. The practice was intended to prevent mistakes and teach humility. Sister Brigid repeatedly reported failures such as breaking a dish, burning food, and spilling soup. One day after several episodes of asking pardon within a short space of time, Sister began yet another report, but she was quickly interrupted by the novice directress who said, "Don't ask for any more penances. You sound like you are bragging!"

Years later Sister Brigid stated that she had so many missteps early on that when a seasoned cook, Sister Thaddea, first met her and greeted her with, "I under-stand you want to be a cook Sister," she immediately exclaimed, "Not any more!"

Fortunately Sister Brigid did persevere and even went on to lead the cook team in both the Ohio and Virginia boarding schools that the Sisters operated.

Organizing and maintaining the large walk-in freezers was difficult. Sheets of cardboard on their cold cement floors were changed periodically when soiled.

The first time Sister Brigid did this, she found herself crawling on the floor between narrow rows of tall shelves loaded with boxes of frozen food items. (All this in a complete floor-length religious habit I might add!) At the rear of the long freezer on a sheet of old cardboard she read a note from a previous cleaner. It said, "You're crazy if you made it this far!!"

Sister did not have to look for trouble. It found her! With her youthful good looks, she miraculously made it to the convent, only to have to put up with a woman chaser working for the grease collecting company.

"The Grease Man" as the Sisters referred to him, came regularly to the kitchen to pick up used grease and oil saved for him in a large barrel kept in the meat cooler. Processed grease would become exotic lotions, make-up, and all sorts of cosmetics. Yes, the Sisters were recycling even then!

You might say that the Grease Man "took a shine" to Sister Brigid. One day when Sister was momentarily alone in the kitchen, he followed her around the kitchen table with daring. He moved closer; she moved away. He moved closer, and she moved away until another Sister providentially walked into the kitchen. Soon after, the convent changed grease companies.

Live and Learn

Sometimes new cooks had difficulty multiplying recipes. Mistakes were made, and the trainer cooks tried to save the day. Sister Mary Rita, an Italian Sister a few years my senior, added enough of one ingredient to multiply her angel food cake recipe many times over. The Sister trainer, not wanting to waste the ingredients

Cook Sisters Mary Stefana, Mary Ann Patrick, and
Sean Maureen

already mixed, proceeded to multiply the remaining
ingredients too. She then pulled every baking pan in the
house to bake off the huge amount of angel food cake.
When Sister Dorotheus returned from being away on
retreat, she saw a great deal of angel food cake. The
Sister trainer explained the "multiplication of the
loaves."

Sister Dorotheus suggested serving it to the sixty
novices, since the hundred and twenty professed Sisters
already had cake. The Sister trainer said, "We did."
"Well, serve it to the forty aspirants and the thirty Sisters
in the infirmary then." "We did." "How about the
twenty-five workmen?" "We did." It turns out everyone
had some angel food cake, and there was still cake on
hand. O happy fault!

New cooks also dealt with the challenge of timing meal "doneness" to correspond to the convent schedule. There were at least a few mealtimes when the whole community sat and waited and waited for the food to be cooked, thus providing lessons in both patience and humility!

Sister Thaddea, with her calm, organized manner, often trained new cooks at the butcher block. Sister had a talent with meat prep and cooking in quantity. One day she was completing the trimming of a half steer into pieces that would be used as roasts, steak, stew, and ground beef. Her apprentice was grinding pieces designated for hamburger.

Beautiful trimmed tenderloin had been set aside at the edge of the butcher block for a special meal of filet mignon for priest guests that evening. However, the apprentice cook, moving along confidently and rather quickly, picked up the piece and held it over the grinder.

"No!!" came the call across the room, but seconds too late! The tenderloin was now ground meat! For some time the "tenderloin Sister" suffered from her mistake as though she wore the scarlet letter.

The art of cooking a pot of meat stock is not always pretty and for some of us downright disturbing! It took me a while to learn my lessons at the meat block and the preparation of soup stock without them eliciting squeamish noises. Seeing knuckle bones floating in a steamy pot and then having someone tell you to put raw egg shells in the broth to clarify it and keep it from clouding does something to you. When Sister Trina said to me one day that we were going to put the pig's tail in with the soup bones, that was it! My response: "Sister Trina, we are not that hungry!"

51

Sister Stefana, a young Sister in her later twenties of Slovenian descent, had a talent for teasing. She heard of my difficulties in regard to pigs' tails and felt I needed to be sensitized to them. That's why she left one in my personal items drawer in the kitchen. I discovered it when I reached in for my prayer book for chapel. I never did get over that!

Getting Caught Up in One's Work

Some Sisters had the habit of being caught up in their work. Sister Thaddea was standing alongside the large, floor model mixer, mashing potatoes. As she leaned over to scrape the sides of the bowl, her long white veil was sucked in by the paddle. She was struggling to reach the power switch when her large black rosary, worn at the side, also slipped in, pulling her even further into the bowl! Thankfully, someone reached the lever to turn off the mixer, and Sister Thaddea was saved from sharing the bowl with mashed potatoes. Talk about food contamination! I believe we served those mashed potatoes, folks.

Then there was the day Sister Stefana turned away from the stovetop to address someone and the tip of her starched white veil swept over the open flame behind her. Immediately Sister caught fire! There was nothing else for the Sister nearest her to do but to rip off the veil and stomp it on the floor. I am not sure what was more humiliating, causing the burning veil or being veil-less.

Fortunately, no cook was directly over the garbage disposal the day when it was turned on, and after a clunky noise was heard, a shiny paring knife shot straight up blade first.

Quoting St. Augustine, the older cooks would say, "Here cut, here burn, but spare me in eternity!" I just know they will be spared in eternity.

Fun Times

Sometimes we just had to lighten things up when work was tiring. On occasion, this found expression in a potholder fight that started small with one or two flying disks across the kitchen and then became all-out warfare when other Sisters joined in. One time a potholder flew over the kitchen wall and hit none other than Sister Christopher, directress of junior professed Sisters, the superior. Oops!

Sister Christopher, looked like the college science professor that she was. A tall and lean figure, she carried herself upright and with an intent gait, her head leading. Sister often had a book or Bible tucked inside her arm at the elbow and held close. She usually wore a studious expression that quickly changed to a warm smile with a glint of humor in her eyes when she greeted you. Sister Christopher was known for her wonderful sense of humor.

After retrieving the potholder that hit her in the hallway, Sister Christopher meandered into the main entrance of the kitchen and merely asked, "Did someone in here lose this?"

Older cooks tell of two Sisters looking for a little levity. They learned the fine art of swinging pails of milk in a complete circle like a wheel, defying gravity and spilling not a drop of milk! I guess this released some tension for them. Apparently not enough because they did not persevere in the convent.

Religious Superiors

The title superior was common in religious life prior to the Second Vatican Council. This title was assigned to a man or woman religious who was deemed a worthy mentor and charged with directing other members of a community. This individual was appointed by a higher community authority. A superior ensured that members were appropriately engaged in ministry in accordance with the religious Rule and the customs of the congregation. She or he was available for guidance and dialogue regarding the spiritual and ministerial challenges met along the way. Where the superior sat in the dining room was known as "first" table.

The Council brought sweeping change to the Church in the modern world, including changes in language. Terms such as local coordinator subsequently replaced superior.

At other times cooks engaged in animated exchanges and uproarious laughter as they worked. Let's just say it. They were loud! This did not go down well with some Sisters who desired a bit more religious decorum. Consequently, one might expect a visit in the kitchen from the local superior who suggested toning it down. (She might be described as the "Mayor of the Provincial House.") On one such an occasion, Sister Julia, in exasperation, spontaneously responded to the admonition, saying, "It's times like this that I wish I had said yes to Andy!"

Cooks were at home during the day when other Sisters were at school. Therefore, occasionally they were asked to help out with certain situations. One such event was placing metallic strips on poles to mark the road to the Motherhouse during a blizzard. As the Sisters trooped through the deep snow, Sister Julia, with characteristic daring, suggested making their way just a little farther to the empty guest house for some hot chocolate, cookies, and TV, which were standard provision for guests. The "guests" that day really appreciated the little respite.

CHAPTER 10

TRADITION! TRADITION!

As novices, we once had the opportunity to go out to the theater to see the movie *Fiddler on the Roof.* What a treat that was! Wonderful music and story. The main character Tevye, a Jewish man, sang about tradition, struggled to keep it, and adjusted to changes that came with time. The Sisters too were pondering their traditions in the 60s with the proclamations of the Second Vatican Council that aimed at renewing the Church in the modern world.

"Tradition" was the operative word when I was a new Sister. Customs ranged from wearing the traditional religious habit to the kinds of meals we served. The latter was a bit overwhelming to me.

Meals were planned using an elaborate system correlated with the Church's liturgical calendar. At the time, I thought that in its details this practice bore a resemblance to Jewish dietary laws. As a cook, I felt I surely would never manage it well.

Essentially the meals for celebrations were categorized into first, second, and third class. First class meals were for celebrating major feasts like Easter, Christmas, and Pentecost or for significant days in community history like Founder's Day. Second class were for less important commemorations. Third class might be for a particular saint's day.

Fortunately this class system was discontinued, allowing us to celebrate special meals in a simpler fashion. I for one could not have been happier.

The cooks excelled in preparing celebratory meals. There were special entrées, chicken being a favorite. Since we did not raise chickens, the meat was purchased. On the other hand, a stuffed pork chop from one of our pigs was also definitely first class.

First class at breakfast meant BACON! Everyone looked forward to it. On the day before celebrating a feast day, pounds of bacon were broiled in a large roaster in the oven and turned with a fork to keep strips separate yet curled until crisp. Bacon was then drained in a large colander and finally laid gently into chafing pans to be warmed before breakfast the following morning. The aroma wafted through the cloister, announcing the next day's feast day. Anticipation is part of enjoyment.

We garnished and decorated for feasts, whereas this was not done ordinarily. Simplicity and poverty were still usually the order of the day. Despite this, meals were attractive.

For example, a first class breakfast often meant half grapefruits that were "flipped," that is, had their sections turned up. It was quite a feat to do 100 plus of these for breakfast! Gelatin salads were a feature. Sister Mary Trina's ribbon jello was possibly the most elaborate. Let's not forget homemade rolls, coffee cakes, and desserts. If we had donated bakery, however, we used this.

For us cooks, a really challenging time would be a series of first class meals—a sure way to "kill the cook."

Celebratory meals were wonderfully tasty and decorative. They complemented other ways the Sisters celebrated: special prayers, skit, and decorations on tables and hanging from ceilings. To this day I like to "flip my grapefruit" and make it pretty.

St. Patrick's Day in Germantown

The coming of spring coincides with the start of the Lenten season for Catholics. If one happens to be of Irish heritage, St. Patrick's Day means a bit of green splashed about an otherwise purple Lenten setting. And so it was at the Notre Dame convent in Chardon, Ohio. However, with the coming of St. Paddy's Day there was a wee bit of conflict for our religious community steeped in German history and customs. At least this was true one particular spring when I was a young Sister. Here is how it unfolded.

One of my friends in the novitiate noticed that St. Patrick's Day was on a Friday in Lent. She figured that at breakfast surely we would all be enjoying white grape juice colored green with food coloring, and this would be accompanied by hot, pork-based Gruitze, since we were permitted to have meat on St. Patrick's Day.

In my simplicity I shared this observation out loud within earshot of Sister Dorotheus. Being of German heritage and not especially enthusiastic about all the Irish hoopla from the many young Irish Sisters of the 60s, Sister stated that she was not happy to hear what was expected with such certainty. In a moment of frustration, and perhaps a bit of ethnic rivalry, she set about to insert variety.

She changed the planned menu of green treats, which, in fact, was then customary on March 17. But wait! Not only did she change the menu, but she planned for oranges to be served at breakfast! ORANGES on St. Patrick's Day! I am guessing my readers probably know what fury the color orange elicits from the Catholic Irishman on St. Paddy's Day.

Lauds Coffee and Convent Silence

Lauds was the morning prayer in the Liturgy of the Hours (Divine Office). Lauds coffee was coffee left from the previous day. It was available in a pot on the kitchen stove. Lauds coffee was consumed by any early birds who felt the need for a caffeine jolt before prayers in chapel.

Silence is a monastic custom intended to foster prayer and contemplation. In the absence of noise and distraction, the religious were better able to focus their entire attention on communing with God. Except for specified periods of recreation, silence was to be maintained in the convent. *Silencium rigorosum* is Latin for "strict silence," which was observed from the end of day (for Notre Dames, this was 9:10 p.m.) up to Lauds, meditation time, and the celebration of the Eucharist in the morning.

The "troubles" started at dawn that day when a very Irish Sister came to the kitchen for a cup of Lauds coffee. This time of morning was still considered the time of *silencium rigorosum* or the Great Silence when talking was not allowed at all. However, this Sister, seeing the large pan of oranges in the scullery ready for breakfast servers to plate and pass to each table, exclaimed, "Oranges on St. Patrick's Day!" Others heard and saw. By breakfast the disturbance was pretty palpable. So, without any delay, the superior, seated at the "first" table, rang the bell!

Convent Bells

In the convent a bell was used to call attention for an announcement to the gathered community. It also signaled the start and ending of prayers and the beginning of silence times. A bell (called click) was rung over the PA system to summon the Sisters to chapel for prayer. Then another bell (called full) was rung to signal the beginning of the prayers.

An old German Sister who had cooked for the seminarians studying at Notre Dame University in South Bend, Indiana, sat next to the superior and whispered to her, "If this happened at Notre Dame, the rector would have sent all the oranges back to the kitchen!" The Sister superior good-humoredly shared this information with the listening community. There was mixed reaction, some not so good! Everyone ate the oranges, but a few folks were stewing, and Sister Dorotheus was a bit upset.

The reality was that many Sisters of other nationalities had joined the immigrant German community that Notre Dame once was in Northeastern Ohio. And a good many of these were spunky Irish!

CHAPTER 11

THE DAY THE CARDINAL CAME FOR LUNCH

The height of etiquette in meal service, Sister Dorotheus informed us, is a pre-plated meal. That was what we would offer when Cardinal John Wright, the highest-ranking American in the Roman Curia, came for lunch! He was to meet with other important clerics at our Motherhouse, which afforded a generous meeting space in a nice country setting. We had the women power to make their meeting comfortable and tasty too. This event was like nothing I had experienced before. There was great excitement and meal planning in detail.

Various items in the meal were to be prepared to near perfection. Each person had a specific extra job in the plating of the meal so that the portion, placement, color contrast, and temperatures of plate and food were just perfect.

My job was to place the parsley garnish. I was new and one of the youngest in the kitchen. The other meal items were safely in the hands of skilled chefs. Frankly, I was relieved by my lowly task. I could take it all in and help the others as needed.

The day arrived. Everything was perfectly falling into place. The dining room was set, carpets had been washed, halls were clean and shiny, and the elevator that the Cardinal would use had been scoured and off limits until after the event.

I am not sure why two cook Sisters determined that they could ride up on that elevator to the kitchen with a few milk cans on the dolly that day, but their trip up went down in infamy. You guessed it. Just three hours before the Cardinal's arrival, three five-gallon milk cans tipped and fell off the dolly inside the elevator onto the floor.

Milk flowed over the edge of the doorway into the shaft below and down the wall. The two Sisters learned what elevator shafts look like up close, as they stared in horror at the river of spilt milk. Theirs was the task to get the milk cleaned up pronto. I think others helped the two culprits, but they led the charge. I recall that a few persons were very displeased about the catastrophe. But when the Cardinal came, he rode up to the dining room in a freshly cleaned, all but new elevator!

While the flooded elevator was one significant cook moment, there were many others, including another elevator-related mishap. The Sisters' college had a dumbwaiter, a device used to send food to other floors. One day a Sister hurriedly opened the door to the dumbwaiter shaft and slid in a tray of pies. Oops! The dumbwaiter cart was still parked on another floor!

Then there was the time that Sisters who were missionaries in India came home and paid a visit to the novitiate. For the occasion, a special Indian meal was prepared for that evening. Unfortunately, on the elevator on the way up to the novitiate, the large container was spilled. Frantic novices scooped up the meal and it was served. No one got sick, probably because every floor in the convent was cleaned every day and kept spotless. We cried about mishaps like these then and laughed about them years later.

CHAPTER 12

HARVESTING THE GARDEN

God said, "I have given you every plant with seeds on the face of the earth, and every tree that has fruit with seeds. This will be your food." ~ Genesis 1:29

The garden on Shamrock Acres, the Sisters' property across Auburn Road, was huge! Or so it appeared to the eyes of this small town nineteen-year-old girl. As a postulant, I joined others in the novitiate planting, weeding, and harvesting the garden. At the peak of the growing season, we often went to the garden even during our recreation time.

I named my section Sean's Share of Shamrock Acres. I kind of took ownership of it in this way. To this day I know where that little patch is located.

One day the novice directress diplomatically suggested to the postulant directress that perhaps the young Sisters could do a little less gardening and a little more baseball, bike riding, walking and talking, or whatever else they wanted in order to relax. Thankfully a balance was found.

The garden was planted with the consultation of Sister Dorotheus and others to determine which veggies and fruits could best be used. Tomatoes and cucumbers provided the community with home-canned stewed tomatoes, sauces, and pickles of every variety. You name it, we had it! We only purchased enough other canned or frozen items to supplement the garden.

Recreation Times

The monastic day was balanced. Times of prayer alternated with periods of work, which was carried out in silence. After lunch and supper, an hour was devoted to recreation, a time for conversing and having fun. As young Sisters, we were bundles of energy! Competitive sports, hiking through the woods, riding a bike up and down the Geauga country hills, and swimming were therapeutic. So were relaxing activities such as playing musical instruments, singing, sewing, taking a leisurely walk outdoors, and playing cards or a game of Backgammon—even if you lost repeatedly! These times fostered camaraderie and friendships to last a lifetime.

Besides working in our own garden, we sometimes went to pick strawberries or other produce offered to the Sisters. One day I was assigned to drive a van of Sisters to Avon, Ohio, to the farm of Sister Mary St. Leo's brother, who had planted a whole field of rhubarb for the Sisters. We also had an annual invitation from the Missionaries of the Precious Blood to pick all the rhubarb that we wanted from their fields at Brunnerdale Seminary in Canton, Ohio. Rhubarb was processed and frozen in numerous three-gallon metal freezer cans for use all year.

Eventually we planted our own rhubarb field, as rhubarb was very much enjoyed and froze well. I had never experienced rhubarb before, but soon it became and remains a personal favorite!

Canning season meant an early start for the day. Work lasted however long it took to "put up" fresh produce as quickly as possible. Only the best produce at its freshest was processed for storage, a standard safe practice for all food preservation. To help with this mission, each day during harvest time the youngest to the oldest cook Sisters could be found sitting side by side down the main hall outside the kitchen.

On one side of each Sister sat the box of fruit or vegetables, and on her opposite side, a pot for the freshly peeled and cut product. On each Sister's lap rested a pan with a peeler or knife. One cook made the rounds, picking up full pots. Off to the canning room she went, where all was processed to be enjoyed all winter long.

Throughout the corridors and billowing out the windows, the sweet aromas of corn relish, stewed tomato, bread and butter pickles, spiced pears, and the like floated in the autumn air. These fragrantly announced the homey activity of canning season at the convent.

Freezing foods eventually took precedence over the home canning process. This resulted in much time saved. I do believe the Sisters were on the frontiers in food preservation, freezing all sorts of fruits and vegetables. We grew bolder in using the freezing process as we experienced success.

CHAPTER 13

OUR LADY OF LOURDES PARISH

SLAVIC VILLAGE

After some training at the Motherhouse, young Sisters were usually sent to the affiliations (smaller communities of Sisters located in parishes or convent schools). Some Sisters remained at the Provincial House, and some eventually returned to it.

In 1973, my first assignment, or "obedience" as it was termed then, was to Our Lady of Lourdes Parish in Cleveland, Ohio, for one year. This was followed by three years at St. John Parish, McLean, Virginia. Then when a need arose at the Notre Dame Academy boarding school in Middleburg, Virginia, I was sent there and remained six years. In 1982, I was assigned to Regina High School, South Euclid, Ohio, for six years and finally, in 1990, to Notre Dame College, South Euclid, Ohio, for five years. In each assignment I learned significant lessons about culinary arts, ministry, and life.

My first year cooking in a small house was a new experience in more ways than one. Our Lady of Lourdes Parish was located at East 55th and Broadway in a section of Cleveland's inner city known as Slavic Village. The neighborhood once had a rich ethnic population of Czech and Bohemian immigrants. These families founded the parish and built the beautiful structure that stands today.

When I arrived in August, there was still a hub of these immigrants. In addition, there was a new influx of families from Appalachia and a significant number of Latinos. St. Alexis Hospital was just down the street, and the area had been a bustling commercial district back in the day. However, most of the prosperous shop owners were gone, and a wind of poverty had swept in. Today efforts for renewal and rejuvenation of the old neighborhoods including this one are underway.

Learning to Shop

At Lourdes, I was able to practice my culinary skills on the small community of five Sisters. Sister Mary Leah was the local superior, while the other Sisters staffed the parish elementary school. Sister Leah was known for her ability to manage, budget, and drive a bargain. It was thought that she would be a good mentor for me on my first assignment outside the Motherhouse.

Sister was one of those "coupon shoppers"—I am sure you've met them—always scanning her collection for super savings. She intended to see that I was trained to shop economically and to plan nutritional menus. Off to the Central Market we ventured, the young Sister and the elderly, still very spry, Sister mentor.

Lesson one: Learn to bargain. At the market Sister said, "Watch me. I want to show you how to bargain with these shrewd vendors." She then approached a man selling grapefruits, asked his price, and instantly feigned shocked at his overcharging. Sister proceeded to scold him. "You should be ashamed of yourself," she told him. "How can you ask a price like that? How do you expect poor people to afford your grapefruits?"

The man initially tried to defend himself, but one could see he was over a barrel, unwilling to get into an argument with an elderly nun. Smiling, he offered, "Just let me know what you would like, and we can get you a good price, Sister!" And he walked away.

Not five minutes later, I heard his booming voice among others as he found his staff eating the fruit on display. I thought for sure there would be a fight. But back to us he came, smiling as if nothing had just occurred. "Have you decided on anything else, Sister?" This was a most colorful first lesson at the Central Market in Cleveland.

City Living

I was a bit fearful of the big city. We heard a lot of noise at night. One evening a couple of cars of young folks had a heated argument outside my third floor bedroom window. I scurried down the hall to ask another Sister to come listen. Then we called the police and waited. About a half hour later the police finally arrived. It was, after all, Friday night in Cleveland. By then the fight had subsided. Fortunately no one was hurt.

Then there was that one Alcoholics Anonymous meeting night at the school directly across from the convent. From my room I heard sirens coming right up to the school cafeteria door. In went the police and rescue squad through the glass door entrance. A short time passed, and out the door came a stretcher bearing a rather large form. A big man, I thought. But the next day the principal told me that a very pregnant woman delivered twins. She had not wanted to miss the AA meeting, which she attended due to her husband's problem.

Again, I was startled one day when the doorbell rang close to noon as I was preparing lunch. The woman at the door wished to engage in conversation about religion. I listened and finally said, "I am sorry but I must finish lunch prep for the Sisters." The visitor said, "Good day," and left. The very next week, didn't she return again! This time I said: "Look at me. Do I look like I need to be converted? (I was in full religious habit.) Perhaps you could find another person who would benefit from your work." She agreed with a smile and did not return.

Sister Leah

Sister Leah wanted me to learn to drive around Cleveland, so she planned trips to various Notre Dame convents in the area whenever an opportunity presented itself. I learned quickly after a few sudden "Turn right here!" commands.

The first time I drove the Shoreway the image that flashed through my mind was "racetrack." "Are you all right, Sister?" Sister inquired as we sped along. "Fine," I replied. I can still feel the texture of that steering wheel as I held tight for dear life.

Sister Leah had a big heart. I learned this almost from day one when she instructed me to expect a visitor each week. He would appear around midafternoon and ask if he might have something to eat.

Mr. Smith was a short, bent over, elderly man, hard on his luck. His clothing was shabby and worn, as were his shoes; but he had a grateful smile as he accepted his hot meal. He sat on the steps inside the convent to eat and then took his bagged dinner for later. When he was finished, he thanked again and said, "God bless you!"

Mr. Smith stopped coming after several months, and I was left to wonder what became of this gentle soul.

—

When I think of the chance we took having him come inside, I can only conclude that the Lord took care of us.

Father Andel was pastor when I arrived. He went mushroom picking each fall, and that year he pulled his car up to the convent, opened his trunk, which was full of mushrooms, and said to me, "Take what you can use." I learned the art of making a good mushroom soup. Not long after, when Father heard we had lots of other Sisters over for a meal and jubilee celebration, he pulled up to the convent again. This time his trunk was full of beer! We enjoyed this at our celebration, and Sister Leah said we could finish up any leftovers later but preferably just before bed.

Each night while the weather was nice, Father would walk back and forth in the parking lot between the convent and rectory, smoking his cigar. One evening Sister Leah went out and walked with him up and down for a long time. She had gone out to talk him into letting go of a disagreement he had with the Sisters. I don't think he ever changed his position on the matter, but he was always good to the Sisters. The two of them walking up and down that evening was a picture.

I did learn quite a bit from Sister Leah. We sat down every two weeks to plan menus and shopping. After awhile she declared, "I think you are just fine doing this on your own," and she turned me loose! She also gave me good advice when she told me not to mix up the eastern European nationalities in Cleveland. "Slovaks are not the same as Slovenians, and Czechs are different from Bohemians," she declared.

Each year the parish would host an ethnic home-coming dinner night complete with Bohemian dumplings, kraut, and blood sausage. My job the following day was to share the leftovers with the other local convents by driving around town and delivering a taste of Bohemia. The dumplings were huge and very tasty, but I would not touch the blood sausage. Perhaps a different name would help!

From one of our neighbors, a woman who sent her children through Lourdes school, I learned of the wonderful combination of noodles and fried cabbage. She also introduced me to kolache and cheesecake just in time for the holidays.

The year at Our Lady of Lourdes convent taught me the skills of menu planning, shopping, time management, and working with food independently. Thank you, Sister Leah! I enjoyed meeting the people of the parish, the Czech-Bohemian hymn singing, the Saturday evening Spanish Mass so full of joy, the lady next door who shared her recipes, the history of each local parish I visited with Sister Leah, and, of course, learning to live with four Sisters much older than I and with widely different interests and backgrounds. That was quite the challenge! At the end of the year, I was ready for a change.

CHAPTER 14

ST. JOHN PARISH

MCLEAN, VIRGINIA

"Sister Sean Maureen, your obedience this year will be at St. John's Parish, McLean Virginia." Those were the words I read on the card in my envelope in chapel on appointment day 1974. It was the custom to receive one's annual ministry in the context of community prayer. Trusting in God's providence and having promised obedience to community authority, the Sisters were missioned to various locations to spread the Good News!

And so I went to St. John Parish, which had a parish school. The community of nine Sisters in the convent there was a mix of ages and ministries. Sisters Mary Nanette, Joele, Antoinette, and John Paul were classroom teachers. Sister Johnmarie taught music, and Sister Marcella was the principal and local superior. Not all Sisters were in the school. Sister Mary St. Leo was a textbook writer, Sister Mary Eduard was the Superintendent of Elementary Schools for the Diocese of Arlington, and Sister Mary Jeannine was the Director of Religious Education in charge of the parish school of religion, as the Confraternity of Christian Doctrine (CCD) came to be called. We all shared the large, modern convent at the end of a stony lane off of Old Dominion Road. Residents did not want the lane paved because then traffic would increase in our quiet neighborhood.

How exciting to be close to Washington, D.C., and yet how deep my homesickness. Now my family could not so easily come see me. I felt the distance between us keenly! Besides, this was only the second year following my younger sister Bonnie's death from a staph infection she acquired while working in a hospital.

Bonnie and I were as close as sisters could be. When I left home for the convent, my mother wrote, "Bonnie walked around like a lost soul!" My sister and I went everywhere and did everything together. She would have loved to see McLean and be close to those Kennedys we were such fans of. That Kennedy connection made McLean very intriguing to me. Ultimately my new community and the thrill of being near the nation's capital won out. Soon, I learned my way around Washington and Northern Virginia.

Car Accidents

I was still sharpening my driving skills, and this proved true on my first trip to National Airport to pick up Sisters arriving by plane from Ohio. Driving into the parking lot, I managed to get too close to the stone pillars at the pay station, resulting in a scratched door. Sister Marcella was not happy to learn this and advised me to try to be more careful as I would be driving around Washington quite a bit. It was quite a while later that the second car mishap occurred. This one Sister Marcella never did hear about or see evidence of. That's right. This little devil did it again!

Sister Marcella, remember that day you asked me to drive you to school because your feet hurt, and you could not bear to walk the gravel road? Going past the garbage

---

73

truck on the left, I inched close to the tree branches, and we heard a screech. You gasped, but I responded, "Everything is fine. We were nowhere near the truck."

We dropped you off at school, and Sister Mary St. Leo and I hurried off to the store. When I got out of the car, I saw the little rubber knobs that held the decorative metal strip that ran alongside the door, but no metal strip! I was terrified, and Sister St. Leo remarked, "Sister Marcella will not be happy. Quick! Let's get what we need and look over the route here. The strip has to be somewhere."

We looked down the road and then went to the bushes where we passed the garbage truck. There the strip was, hanging from the bushes! I had the strip but could still expect an admonition of some proportions. As we returned to the convent garage, Sister St. Leo said, "I will pray for you, Sister!" Then she rushed in to meet a writer's deadline.

I stood by the car and looked at the rubber knobs on the side. I looked at the strip of chrome. Hmmm. Only slightly bent and looked like it just snapped on. I tried it. Yay! It worked! I rushed up to Sister St. Leo's office and asked her to come down to see how I fixed the car. She was shocked to see a normal driver's door with chrome decoration. Neither of us breathed a word, and no one ever noticed the ever so slight curve in the chrome strip. That was my last car event, Sister Marcella. Honest!

New Interests

I also enjoyed testing my cooking talents, and the Sisters at St. John's enjoyed the meals. (At least I think they did!) I even taught baking to the eighth grade girls at the principal's request. Unfortunately Sister Marcella came home that evening and declared, "Do you know what your baking class did with their cream puffs? They had a food fight on the bus. No more baking classes!"

My primary role in McLean alongside preparing meals for the nine Sisters in residence could be described as Catering Sister or at least a point person for events involving food. There were about seventy-five Sisters of Notre Dame in Northern Virginia in those years, and the region gathered regularly. Most times everyone brought some part of the meal. Other times I prepared the works, and folks could just come and enjoy.

It was at St. John's that I experienced a spurt of creativity. For recreation I dabbled in Baker's Clay, a salt dough used to make knickknacks. I baked little Betsy Clark type dolls. Next I discovered the art of quilling, rolling up thin strips of paper to form objects. This too caught my fancy. Soon followed wood circles on which quotations were scripted in black ink. In between these projects, I taught myself to play the guitar.

I had some time to spare and wanted to try my hand at more creative ventures. Sister Mary Joele planned to take a watercolor painting class in D.C. She talked of painting scenes along the Potomac River on Saturdays, which sounded very good to me. Sister saw my interest and suggested I ask to take the art class as well. We could both attend and that would be fun. But in those years, cook Sisters just did not become involved in educational pursuits, much less in order to foster an art hobby. Because I would not be using this art education, I was not granted the permission to take the class.

The encouragement and friendship of the Sisters at St. John's fostered in me an inner strength and confidence. I learned to trust myself. My takeaway from my time in McLean was that I discovered my creative tendencies, new talents, and how I enjoy learning and trying new things. I applied this discovery to my culinary work (but also kept alive my interest in other arts). I always liked to bake. But then I realized that I also had a special talent for creating meat dishes.

I should have paid more attention to you, Sister Joele. In those years I was stuck in meat, potatoes, and cheese. You kept saying: "Do more veggie dishes." You were ahead of the times. Remember the day I made Baked Alaska with you and Sister Nanette for Sister Mary Christopher's visit? It was memorable. The rest of the community sang "When It's Springtime in Alaska" as the dessert melted on its way to the table. I should try this recipe again sometime.

In summary, at St. John's I expanded my cooking experiences to include quite a bit more variety, especially in regard to baking and large event planning. The community was more diverse, and some Sisters were closer in age to me than my previous one, which was helpful. The opportunity and excitement of traveling about D.C. left lasting memories.

I especially remember meeting Archbishop Fulton J. Sheen. Sister Joele and I ran from the church down the back steps to the hall beneath the Arlington St. Thomas Cathedral. No, we did not trample anyone! We were simply ahead of the crowd to meet him. Literally we were first to greet and shake his hand. My McLean years left me with fond memories and a good measure of adventure near our nation's capitol.

CHAPTER 15

NOTRE DAME ACADEMY

MIDDLEBURG, VIRGINIA

Help was needed in the boarding school kitchen of Notre Dame Academy (NDA), an all-girl high school in Middleburg, Virginia, and I was chosen to fill the spot. I said goodbye and left my little kitchen in the suburbs of Washington for the larger kitchen in Middleburg.

The St. John McLean community had become my friends. I had planted Evening Primrose in the backyard. Now I wouldn't be there to watch them open each evening. Hebrews 13:14 became the focus of my meditation: "We have here no lasting home!" Sisters went where ministry and obedience called.

Driving up the winding entrance road to Notre Dame Academy, I viewed the school sitting high on a hill overlooking the mountains. I felt the certain mystique that was Middleburg. Down the road from the Academy was "the house that Jackie built," a yellow bungalow designed for the first family when John Kennedy was in the White House. Farther down the way was the home of Liz Taylor Warner, who, I was told, often shopped in the little town of Middleburg on weekends. Around the bend was Upperville, home of Peter Marshall, famous preacher, author, and one time chaplain to the U.S. Senate. For sure, I was fascinated with my new assignment, but a little scared too!

The Sisters of Notre Dame no longer operate Notre Dame Academy. However, the memory of this idyllic school in the awesomely beautiful "hunt country" fifty miles west of Washington, D.C., lingers in the heart.

There, the Sisters served as educators for daughters of foreign and domestic diplomats, congressmen, national newscasters, Georgetown professors, and Washington Redskin coaches! Students were not only from Northern Virginia and Washington, D.C., but from across the U.S.A. Some came from faraway countries like Nicaragua and Aruba.

Notre Dame Academy girls graduated on a day in May during a formal ceremony. As is customary in the South, carrying a dozen red roses, they gathered at the

—

main house on the balcony and grand staircase, which was like the one in the movie *Gone with the Wind*. Pictures were taken, and then the slow march to the auditorium began. Over the breezeway, the mountains in view, they marched to "Pachelbel's Canon" with piano and other instrumental accompaniment. The graduates processed ever so slowly, so all could take in this special moment.

Middleburg was horse country where equestrians held their horseshows. A training track for Derby favorites was right next door to the Academy. Around dawn on any good weather morning it was an easy walk to see these magnificent animals get their exercise. One need only follow the sound of hooves and the snort of horses running. The Academy also boarded horses. Equestrian classes were part of the curriculum in the early days of the Academy but eventually were discontinued.

And what was my role in this wonderland? I joined my efforts with three other Sisters and a hardworking lay staff to provide meals. We endeavored to meet the nutritional needs of the 200 girls (100 day students and 100 boarders). Initially, I assisted in the kitchen and then for several more years was Foodservice Director. Over the course of my years there, I worked with Sisters Mary Dorotheus, Brigid, Antonmarie, Stefana, Trina, and Ann Patrick.

We wrote our own menus, purchased wholesale and local fresh foods, and cooked many dishes from scratch. The girls had a fondness for some prepared food, and we could not deny them. One such item comes to mind: Wing Dings! We had ample opportunity to be creative, offering fine dining and a wide variety of meals to keep the teenage girls happy and healthy.

At times, the young ladies were like Oliver in the movie by that name, begging, "I would like more, S'tir." (S'tir was short for Sister.) They would present themselves at the Dutch door entrance to the dining room and ask for two or three more helpings of pasta. Never mind the meatballs! When we attempted to teach the students moderation, the usual response was, "Sister! We pay a lot of money to come here, and we should be allowed to eat as much as we want!"

Though many students came from wealthy or well-known families, at the "Burg" they were just your typical high school girls, gaining a solid education while being fostered in a Catholic environment. No one escaped Sister Seton's instruction to clean up the interior of the van after a long trip to one of the boys' academies for football games or dances. Not even after proclaiming: "Sister, I have maids at home who do this!" Nor were any girls spared being assigned to dishwashing after supper.

The usual scene at breakfast: The double doors to the student dining room open. Out steps Sister Annfrancis. "What's our motto?" she asks. Students respond with the answer they know they must give before plowing into breakfast: "Waste not, want not!!"

There were many humorous, warmhearted moments at NDA and some difficult ones. Cook Sisters worked long hours after special events like dinner dances or the Country Fair, or just getting the new season's menus written. It was one such late night that crossing the breezeway back to the convent, I encountered a large snake over the mantle of the entrance door. Sister Naomi, another brave Sister, came by and together we dealt with the snake. In the process, we woke up a few Sisters whose rooms were above the entranceway.

During another late night at the Burg a break-in to the dorm occurred. Turned out the criminals were a few scrawny freshmen boys from town who did this on a dare. They were caught by the police as they escaped down the road along Goose Creek. I think the biggest scare was hearing gunshots when Sister John Albert shot a gun into the air. She just wanted to scare the intruders that night, which she did—and everyone else too!

Later, the intruders were as polite as could be as they worked off their sentence landscaping in the summer.

Our Dog, Lady

An outcome from the break-in was acquiring a watchdog, Lady. She guarded the delivery area behind the kitchen. Lady was a great watchdog. However, if you wore slacks or if she could not see your legs, she determined that you were a man and wanted to sink her teeth into you! We conjectured that perhaps she was abused by a man in her younger days. One thing for sure: when Lady was tethered, she was on guard and no one dared get near her. Her growl was chilling!

All Lady asked was to be walked in the evenings and sometimes midday. This was sometimes the task of the kitchen Sisters, an assignment that we all enjoyed. Since we were in the country, we walked her off leash. But then one day Lady spotted the father of a student walking up the breezeway entrance to the school and dashed for his ankle. No more off leash!

The bond that developed between dog and caregiver made parting difficult at the end of the school year when Sisters left for the summer, some of them for good. Lady became very depressed and would turn her back when the goodbye morning came. She just knew when this was happening. She stayed in the back of her house with her back toward the entrance. We caregivers had an equally hard time!

Dogs have feelings. This I know. Lady was a special treat for me. She passed away a year or so after I left the Burg and is buried on the school grounds. I expect to see her in heaven. I understand the words of aviator Wiley Post, "If dogs don't go to heaven, I want to go where they go!"

The Kitchen Cats

To be fair, I must tell you that we also had two kitchen cats. One was Catechesis, appropriately named by the Sisters who were studying catechetics in the summertime. She was a pregnant stray who happened to have a litter on the Sisters' back porch. Of course, some of us came to the rescue and eventually found homes for all but Catechesis and one of her sons, Chucky Honey. These two managed to stay outdoors most days and were mousers indoors at other times. When the health inspector arrived on campus, there was a lot of hushed communication to ensure that neither feline made an appearance!

Catechesis loved to perch on a windowsill outside to watch Sister working at the meat slicer just inches away. But for the windowpane, that ham was so close! This cat's cuteness earned her treats!

As for Chucky Honey, he loved to keep me company at night in the kitchen office. While I hammered away at new menus or grocery statements, he lay on top of the desk, watching for any opportunity to steal the show and get his tummy rubbed.

To ice skate, I once tramped through the snowy horse pasture down to a frozen pond by the house of Mr. Lavin, the caretaker. Chucky Honey followed me and then climbed a tree to sit and watch me skate!

How does your heart not warm toward these furry little beasts? Cats are thoughtful and curious, both qualities denoting intelligence. All of us kitchen Sisters and Sister Joseph Frank, the housekeeper, took great comfort from their presence and entertaining ways. And we had no mice!

As for the NDA graduates who are out in the wide world now with their own careers and families, hopefully they are remembering good meals, good education, and good times at NDA, Middleburg, Virginia.

Quantity food production and fine dining were my focus at Middleburg's NDA. Being there educated me in other ways. There was interaction with students from all over the world, including daughters of opposition families in the Nicaraguan conflict. And there was Mr. Tipps, the homeless man who lived in a shack near the horse training track and hitched rides to town with the Sisters when he spotted their cars or vans. I learned the value of a minute in the Monday morning grocery shopping trips to town. At one time there were only two of us cooks. One stayed to get lunch started, and the other shopped in a hurry!

The NDA house had formerly been the Hitt Mansion owned by the powerful and wealthy Hitt family. Robert R. Hitt was a close friend of Abraham Lincoln who became an Illinois congressman. His son William resided in the Virginia mansion. No doubt the Hitts would be pleased that their property was put to such good use.

CHAPTER 16

REGINA HIGH SCHOOL

SOUTH EUCLID, OHIO

After six years at the Academy and a wonderful final summer in Middleburg, providing meals for a group of thirty to forty religious Sisters doing graduate work in theology, I was off to Regina High School, in South Euclid, Ohio. Yet, I keep the memory of the beauty of the Bull Run Mountains off in the distance behind NDA, Middleburg.

The change in state scenery was significant. Northern Virginia was breathtaking in its great natural beauty. Northeastern Ohio, not so much! At one time Regina overlooked an apple orchard that was a sight to behold in the spring, but it had been cut down after the caretaker, August Siemer, could no longer work. The Sisters' residences were also a contrast.

At the Burg, the fifteen or so Sisters resided in a beautiful southern mansion only slightly modified for the Notre Dame community. On the other hand, Regina was a very plain, brown brick building more utilitarian than architecturally significant. About twenty Sisters lived on the second floor of the high school, and therefore were always present at the school.

Regina was an all-girl Catholic high school located in the eastern suburb of South Euclid. Enrollment was around three hundred, about half of what it was in previous years. Formerly, the student body was primarily

Catholic and upper middle class from South Euclid and adjacent suburbs. In the 1980s many students hailed from the city of Cleveland and outlying suburbs as well. The busses rolled in, and Regina was one big happy family! In fact, that was their theme in those years: We Are Family, the name of a current popular song.

The kitchen was on the ground floor just off the maintenance area, and a short hall was a direct link to the coffee source for the custodians. Chief custodian was Hampton Posey, while Paul Bacho and Scott Rendlesham completed the staff.

Mr. Posey, longtime Regina custodian

A cookie jar was prominently displayed on top of the wooden table covered with a tablecloth. It appeared to be a baker's table from the earlier days at Regina when cooks like Sister Mary Eymard and Sister Mary Emmet (now Sister Julia Surtz) ran a full-blown cafeteria for the students. When I arrived, the food source for the students was vending machines. Sandwiches, Twinkies, pieces of fruit, and the like sat on stacked shelves that turned like a merry-go-round, tempting the buyer through the glass windows. This was no replacement for a hot lunch or salad bar!

While my environment changed starkly, so did my job description. We did not have to feed two hundred girls as at the Burg. Instead Sister Marie Bernadette, an elderly Sister, and I just prepared the Sisters' meals, which were delivered on carts to their third floor dining room via elevator. We also assisted with food-related school activities. We merely ordered food and supplies for special events such as Mother Daughter Night, Father Daughter Night, Regina High Day, and the spaghetti dinner fundraiser.

Just as in McLean, with extra time on my hands I filled the void with pursuits that piqued my curiosity. This round it happened to be winemaking and cheesemaking. I thought about learning to make beer, but let that one go.

I did say yes to the home economics teacher who asked me to illustrate for her students how homemade biscuits are made. I also accepted an invitation to demonstrate the craft of cheesemaking to Sister Muriel's chemistry class. I attempted to make Farmer's cheese, a type of cream cheese, and cheddar.

Winemaking

By far my most adventurous pursuit, and successful I might add, was making Vino Regina, a homemade Concord grape wine. The fruit of the vine was produced with the wonderful grapes from the Sisters' vineyards in Chardon.

By Easter that year, each Sister at Regina who wished had a little bottle of Vino Regina to take with them for holiday visits with family and friends. Sister Megan's mom, Mrs. Dull, told me that my first attempt tasted like a good Burgundy! (She was very kind.)

One very early October morning as Mr. Posey walked into the kitchen to pour himself a cup of coffee, he noticed an unusual smell. Impossible, he thought. It smells like alcohol in here! He followed his nose to the Sisters' storeroom door. This was definitely alcohol with a very fruity fragrance.

When I appeared in the kitchen to prepare for breakfast before morning prayers and daily Mass in the school chapel upstairs, Mr. Posey greeted me, shaking his head in disbelief. He said, "Sister Sean, in all my years working here I have never come in to smell alcohol in the Sisters' kitchen. Are you brewing something back there?" I nodded yes, laughing, as I opened the door to reveal my still. There it was, a big 30-gallon rubber drum full of crushed grapes. I explained the process since he was very curious.

In due time I had a five-gallon narrow neck jug brewing with all the proper equipment attached. At first fermentation I had the jug inside a kitchen sink. On Mother Daughter Night a group of ladies was working with refreshments in the kitchen when I received an intercom call in the Sisters' residence. "Sister! Hurry down here. The wine is blowing up and overflowing in the sink!" I went right down and made an adjustment, explaining that the first fermentation of wine can be very exuberant.

In the following weeks, things quieted down as the wine settled and clarified. The juice began looking more and more like vino. Periodically I had to siphon the clearing wine from one jug to another with a rubber hose. This separated it from the settled "must," the sediment of grape solids.

Paul Bacho's seven- or eight-year-old daughter, Jennifer, would often come from her house near Regina and visit with the Sisters in the kitchen. Sometimes we gave her little jobs, which pleased her, and she chatted away.

One day while I was siphoning in the backroom, I was having trouble. Jennifer walked in to see what I was doing. She watched as I gulped the juice a few times, attempting to restore the flow by suction. After about five minutes, Jennifer said, "Sister, you are going to get sick!" I took a break and said, "Jennifer, I think you better go home now. Time for us to go to chapel."

No sooner had she left then Sister Marie Bernadette came in. "You don't look so good," she exclaimed. I didn't feel so good either. In fact, Sister walked me down the hall to the elevator and accompanied me to the Sisters' residence. When the elevator doors opened, I was very dizzy. I wondered if I would "flip my cookies."

Sister took me to my room and said, "I will tell Sister Mary Donald you went to bed sick and check on you later." The last thing I remember as I lay on my bed was the ceiling going around in circles. Time for me to get a real job!

The National Lunch Program

Fortunately, the principal, Sister Mary Barbara Piscopo, and others had an idea to reinstate the hot lunch program so popular in the years before vending machines charmed everyone. The Cleveland Catholic Diocese had a department that oversaw the National Lunch Program in many if not most of the diocesan schools. They would set up the program in a school, but they needed a manager. That's where I came in!

So a team under the leadership of Rene Weber came to Regina to get us started. The program was explained, all equipment provided, and staff was hired. At Regina, a significant number of students qualified for free or subsidized meals.

We featured a salad bar, which was a new food trend at the time. This was a huge success. We enjoyed a supply of many government commodities: cheese, peanut butter, flour, as well as meats like turkey roasts, chicken and beef. Therefore we had the opportunity to provide wonderfully filling and nutritious meals and keep food costs down.

The students were thrilled, we made a nice profit, and everyone was happy.

I must not fail to mention what I think is the greatest benefit of the National Lunch Program. Students who have modest and very poor economic situations are eligible for free or subsidized meals. In the absence of this benefit, some students would surely fall behind for sheer lack of energy, a result of inadequate nutritional intake. I was very pleased to be a part of this program.

Members of our regular cafeteria staff were Sister Marie Bernadette, Rose Cichella, Marge Selan, Pat Bacho, and Karen Mansi. They made it all happen

Rose Cichella, Sister Marie Bernadette, Karen Mansi, Marge Selan, Sister Sean Maureen, and Pat Bacho

successfully every school day for many years—truly an accomplishment to be very proud of.

After we were going along nicely, I was asked to assist for a short time at Padua Franciscan High School as they made some changed in their style of foodservice for the students.

When I arrived on site, I passed through the study hall in session in the school's huge cafeteria. I noticed heads up and turning as students' eyes followed me all the way through the room. Inside the kitchen I remarked on this. The principal, a Franciscan friar wearing the traditional brown habit, explained, "They have not seen a religious Sister in a habit before. One student asked if you were an Amish woman." There you have it! An example of the religious cultural change underway in the late 1980s.

With my involvement in the National Lunch Program, I learned a great deal more about foodservice management, hiring, training staff, and making a profit. I began to think about going back to school to pursue the nutrition part of my foodservice path.

One day Sister Muriel brought Chuck Roscoe, whose daughter was at Regina, to the kitchen to see me. He and I had attended John F. Kennedy High School at the same time. He was now executive chef at Quinn's Restaurant (no relation to me), in Solon, Ohio. Later Sister Muriel, his former teacher, and I were his guests at the restaurant. Mr. Roscoe toured the Regina cafeteria and school storeroom and then exclaimed: "Don't let anyone tell you otherwise. You are virtually running a restaurant here." I kind of thought so!

With the encouragement of the school foodservice personnel at the Cleveland Diocese, I received a small scholarship from the American School Foodservice Association. This was applied to my educational costs that followed. The scholarship marked the first step toward formal education not only in culinary arts and foodservice but in the science of nutrition.

Beginning formal training would be a huge leap for an ND cook. In doing so, I would fulfill the dream of Sister Magdalae (now Sister Theresa Gebura), who, besides encouraging me to be creative, worked to make our foodservice ministry more professional. Her efforts to break out of long-held customs included speaking up, which earned her a few scars. In a way, Sister's dream became my dream.

CHAPTER 17

NOTRE DAME COLLEGE
SOUTH EUCLID, OHIO

Teilhard de Chardin, S.J., once said, "Do not forget that
the value and interest in life is not so much to do
conspicuous things as to do ordinary things with the
perception of their enormous value." By the 80s I had
been "getting the meal on the table" for about ten years
and happily so. I knew the importance of my work.

But Chardin also said, "Our duty as men and women
is to proceed as if the limits to our abilities did not exist.
We are collaborators in creation." I began to sense I had
something more within me—some other capacities to
develop. I thought about my sister Bonnie's disbelief
about my becoming a cook and a friend's wonderment
that my range of ministry was only within community
foodservice. So, what about taking up Chardin's
challenge and examining the limits of my abilities?

I asked the community superiors if I could go back to
school to pursue the science of nutrition and obtain a
degree in dietetics. As a result, that year my obedience
read, "Student at Notre Dame College." More than
"doing ordinary things," I was about to learn the
enormous value of good nutrition in the field of health
care. There was one stipulation: I was to manage
foodservice at Providence Hall, the Sisters' residence at
the College. I would work with cooks Sister Mary Lewis
and Sister Eileen Marie.

After I moved into Providence Hall, I was sometimes asked, "What is it like living with all those college professors, deans, and even the president of Notre Dame College?" This question perhaps was based on the usual image of professors: That when they spoke one needed a dictionary to understand them. It was probably assumed that they couldn't possibly be down to earth, easy to please, and lighthearted. But they were! Besides, they were kind and encouraging to this forty-year-old student.

Sister Jeanmarie DeChant, my chemistry professor, will never fully realize how much it meant when she cheered me on with a "You can do it" in my chemistry and statistics courses! And Sister Mary Frederic kept insisting, "Get a teaching certificate! Go a little further!"

The community was blessed with a wonderful superior, Sister Mary Jonathan Zeleznick, who served her Sisters well. My favorite superior!

Some Sisters whose ministry was not related to the College were also in residence there. This variety of missions, or jobs, made for interesting table conversations.

One resident, Sister Mary Kathleen Glavich, was the editor and author of religious textbooks for schools nationwide and an accomplished author of many other books. Today she is the kind editor of this, my memoir/cookbook.

Sister Catherine Rennecker was the proficient secretary and typist for a Notre Dame textbook series. Then she became our community housekeeper and seamstress and helped all of us out. Sister Catherine and I made our final vows in the same year. I was the youngest of our vow group, while she— a widow who had two grown sons!—was the oldest.

Formation of a Sister of Notre Dame

In my day, a woman who desired to become a Notre Dame Sister spent at least eight years in initial formation before making final vows—far more years than most women are engaged! During these years, the woman hoping to someday be a senior professed Sister (under perpetual vows) strove to deepen her relationship with Jesus especially through prayer.

She was a postulant for a year (or half a year if she had been an aspirant or "prep" during high school). Then she was a novice for two years. One of these years is called "canonical" and is devoted to studying the community. At the end of the novitiate, the novice made temporary vows, which were renewable for five years. She was known as a junior professed. The last six months of the juniorate were spent intensely preparing for final vows, and the woman was known as a tertian.

Sister Mary Roman, a registered nurse, was the retired Dean of Nursing at Case Western Reserve University and coordinated health care needs of Sisters. One Fourth of July I wanted to watch the fireworks against the Cleveland skyline. Running down an embankment at Lakeside Park in Willowick, I stumbled on uneven ground and broke my ankle. I saw stars but no fireworks! Sister Roman and I had quite a discussion about whether I should go to the Motherhouse to heal my broken ankle or stay behind and manage it at the college. She let me win! I stayed home.

If there was anything you needed in the notions department, or, let's just say it, ANYTHING at all, Sister Mary Rochelle had it in her room or would find it for you. This included a small television that she loaned me after I broke my ankle. Her generosity enabled me to follow the O.J. Simpson car chase and trial with Sister Freddie as my TV guest.

There were many other Sisters at Providence, but one who must be remembered was the oldest, Sister Mary Veronica. On any given day, no matter the weather, she could be found going out for her daily Rosary walk. When I asked what her secret was for staying well and agile at 100 years, "The Rosary walk," was her reply.

It was exciting to study again as much as it was scary, wondering how I could do this. But I did it against so many odds. I had just celebrated 25 years as a religious Sister, when, after five years, I finally graduated in 1996 with a B.S. degree in nutrition.

During this time there were many trips home. My mother was declining and in a nursing home. In 1996, her two brothers, my uncles, were beaten up and left for dead in the parish parking lot following Christmas midnight Mass. A mob hit, I was told. I became my uncles' advocate. Eventually these factors contributed to a major change in my life.

CHAPTER 18

LONG TERM CARE

Because I felt a desire to minister beyond the community of Sisters, I requested permission to seek a position in healthcare foodservice outside my religious community. When I got the green light, in 1996, while still a Sister living at Notre Dame College, I began working in long term care at a brand new facility near to Notre Dame College, The Greens of Lyndhurst. This was a Communicare of Ohio Healthcare Campus. I was morning cook/supervisor and experienced the growth of foodservice in healthcare there from zero residents to about a hundred.

In the next two years, I began the work needed to become a Dietetic Technician Registered (D.T.R.) through Cuyahoga Community College. As a result, I gradually moved from actual cooking, to supervising food production, to kitchen management in a healthcare environment, and finally to nutritional assessment and nutritional care.

After almost three years at The Greens, in 1998, I obtained another position: Director of Foodservice at the Villa Sancta Anna Home for the Aged in Beachwood, Ohio. This was a long-established Catholic nursing home owned and operated by the First Catholic Slovak Ladies Association. After seven years, leadership changed, and the corporate owners chose to close this facility.

Life's changes led me to be on leave from my religious community, and I spent significant time caring

for elderly members of my family. My mother died in
2001. Eventually I returned to secular life.

As I searched for another job, in 2005, a professional
contact of mine informed me of a directorship opening in
a small, family-owned nursing home in Newbury, Ohio.
The home firmly espoused Christian principles, a
characteristic that was very important to me. It is here at
Holly Hill Nursing Home, Assisted Living and
Rehabilitation Campus in Geauga County that I have
ministered as Director of Nutrition Services for the last
ten years. Ironically, Holly Hill is located "just around
the corner" from Notre Dame Provincial Center! For me,
the best part of my job is interacting with residents.

George Ohman, Jr., owner and administrator of Holly Hill
Nursing Home and Assisted Living, and Mary Ann Quinn,
Director of Nutrition Services

God's Guidance

I woke up one day and found that I was a nutrition professional specializing in long term care. How did I get here, I asked myself, because I never saw it coming in my youth. I looked back and realized that I was always being formed for this career. I picked up tools along the way: both culinary skills and ministerial skills.

In my formative years as a novice, I learned that God is at work guiding us like a shepherd guides his sheep. It is the Good Shepherd who will make our paths straight and will guide us home should we lose our way. He has a mission for each of us and will see that we carry it out if we but seek his help. My journey from the convent farm to the dietary department in a nursing home was a journey in his company.

Just as the story of the feeding of five thousand with five loaves and two fish held special meaning earlier in my foodservice career, Our Lord's words to Peter: "Feed my lambs. Feed my sheep" hold special meaning in these later years.

SOME DEFINITE SERVICE

Many years ago Sister Mary Christopher shared with the
young Sisters in her care John Henry Cardinal Newman's
reflection "Some Definite Service." It was published in
his book *Meditations and Devotions* in 1848. Today his
words hold new meaning for me and certainly for those
to whom I now minister.

God knows me and calls me by my name....
God has created me to do Him some definite service;
He has committed some work to me
    which He has not committed to another.
I have my mission—I never may know it in this life,
    but I shall be told it in the next.

Somehow I am necessary for His purposes...
    I have a part in this great work;
I am a link in a chain, a bond of connection
    between persons.
He has not created me for naught. I shall do good,
    I shall do His work;
I shall be an angel of peace, a preacher of truth
    in my own place, while not intending it,
    if I do but keep His commandments
    and serve Him in my calling.

Therefore I will trust Him.
    Whatever, wherever I am,
    I can never be thrown away.
If I am in sickness, my sickness may serve Him;
In perplexity, my perplexity may serve Him;
If I am in sorrow, my sorrow may serve Him.

My sickness, or perplexity, or sorrow may be
necessary causes of some great end,
which is quite beyond us.

He does nothing in vain; He may prolong my life,
He may shorten it;
He knows what He is about.
He may take away my friends,
He may throw me among strangers,
He may make me feel desolate,
make my spirits sink, hide the future from me—
still He knows what He is about. ...
Let me be Thy blind instrument. I ask not to see—
I ask not to know—I ask simply to be used.

☙

Clearly my "some definite service" has been to cook.

PART II

Notre Dame Recipes and More

The following recipes were compiled from memory and a little research. Also, I met with a group of cook Sisters who recalled both the stories in this book and favorite food customs. This meeting provided all of us with many warm memories and a great deal of laughter.

Notre Dame Pork Gruitze

We start with a traditional recipe from the rich German history of the Notre Dame congregation. See chapter 2, page 22 for a picture of Gruitze.

Serves 24 (3 ounces each).

3-4 pounds of fresh pork shoulder (blade in)
2   teaspoons salt
2   teaspoons black pepper
2   small onions
1   tablespoon ground sage
2   gallons water (about)
1-2 pounds of medium pearled barley

Rinse pork under cool water and place into a 2-gallon ovenable stewpot. Add spices and one onion. Cover with water and lid.

Bring to boil over medium flame, uncover partially, and reduce to simmer. Cook until the meat is tender and pulls away from the bone with a fork.

Strain the meat, collecting the broth below by using a colander inside a large stainless steel bowl or pot. Cool the stewed pork. Pick the lean meat free of bone, etc. Force the solid lean meat through a meat grinder on the second holes (as we did!) or process to a puree or paste using a food processor. Add the other onion to the grinder or processor. Introduce the ground pork back into the kettle of broth on the stovetop. Stir in.

Popularity of Gruitze

Some Sisters living in smaller communities missed having Gruitze for breakfast. Sisters Julia Surtz at Regina High School and Mary Theresa Gebura at the Provincial Center cooked extra large batches to make it available to them too.

Preheat oven to 300°.

Bring kettle of broth with pork to a boil, and then stir in barley. Add spices and adjust to taste. The mixture should taste of sage and onion and be slightly salty with a hint of heat from the black pepper.

Place uncovered pot into preheated oven and stir every 15 to 20 minutes. The moisture desired will differ according to individual preference and fat content of pork. Pork shoulder should afford a good moisture level. (If pork loin was used, there would be a drier product.) If mixture appears too wet, you may stir in a bit more pearled barley.

Bake in oven about 1½ hours. Barley swells, and mixture will have a pudding-like consistency when finished. Pour Gruitze into a 9 x 13-inch baking pan to cool. Then cover with plastic wrap and refrigerate. Serve next day.

To serve a group at breakfast, partially cover the pan with foil, then reheat in preheated 325° oven for approximately 45 minutes. Ladle 3 to 4-ounce scoops side by side on a meat platter to pass at table.

After making Gruitze a few times, one will achieve the desired balance of moisture, barley, and seasoning.

Baked Breakfast Custard

Breakfast followed Morning Prayer, meditation, and Mass. The Sister who was assigned breakfast that day would place custard in a very slow oven. (Usually set at 200° to 225° to allow for the long chapel time.) Time and temperature adjustments could become tricky when the priest came late for Mass due to snow!

Serves 12 to15.

8   cups milk (whole)
8   eggs (medium)
1   teaspoon salt
1   teaspoon black pepper

Lightly grease a 9 x 13-inch baking pan or casserole dish. Crack 8 eggs into a 4-quart bowl and beat slightly with a French wire whip until blended. Add 8 cups milk and seasonings to the eggs and beat again.

Pour custard into the baking pan and set the pan on a cookie sheet with edges. Bake this in a preheated 325° oven for 30 to 40 minutes or until knife inserted comes out clean.

Variations:
• Add bacon bits, cheese, and sausage to custard.
• Sweetened and flavored with real vanilla, this makes a delicious dessert as well. Thus custard pie!

French Toast

Donated day-old French bread from Hough Bakery and
Orlando Bakery made this a favorite breakfast and easy
to prepare. We soaked the bread in custard the night
before and kept it in the refrigerator. We fried it just
before breakfast. What a treat with maple syrup and
butter!

Serves 6 (1 slice each).

6   eggs
1½ cups milk
½   teaspoon cinnamon (or ½ teaspoon real vanilla)
1   tablespoon sugar
1   pinch of salt
6   slices of French bread cut on an angle ½ inch thick
Cooking oil as needed

Beat eggs, adding milk, sugar (premixed with cinnamon),
pinch of salt, and vanilla (if preferred to cinnamon) until
all is blended, forming custard.
    Soak bread in custard on one side and flip to other
side. Then place soaked bread in a 9 x 13-inch baking
pan, stacking as needed. Pour remaining custard over the
pan of bread. Cover and refrigerate overnight.
    In the morning, oil the fry pan or griddle and heat to
375°. Fry the soaked bread until golden, allowing the egg
to cook on one side. Flip bread over and fry until the
other side is golden and the egg inside the thick bread is
cooked, 1 to 2 minutes each side. The bread will puff up
somewhat when done. Serve immediately with syrup and
margarine pats.

Sister Dorotheus's Waffles

When I worked with Sister Dorotheus in Middleburg, she prepared some wonderful dishes for the small community of Sisters, while the rest of us cooks provided meals for the students, both boarders and day. What a delicious treat waffles were early in the morning before The Charge! Sister always made them light as a feather. She said the secret was alternating the flour, eggs, and buttermilk.

Serves about 5 (10 waffles).

4 eggs
2 cups flour
1 teaspoon salt
1 teaspoon baking soda
1 teaspoon baking powder
2 cups buttermilk (or 1 cup sour cream and 1 cup milk)
1 cup melted butter
Cooking oil for waffle iron

Beat eggs. Add melted butter to buttermilk. Mix by alternating flour, eggs, and buttermilk. Begin and end with flour mixture. Grill in waffle iron that is oiled and hot as per iron directions for about 7 minutes. Serve with syrup or favorite topping.

Sister Mary Anthon's Buttermilk Waffles

This recipe from Sister Mary Anthon (now Sister Mary Janet Kondrat) requires a little extra work, but it is so worth it.

Serves about 5 (10 waffles).

1½ cups sifted all purpose flour
1   tablespoon sugar
1   teaspoon baking powder
1   teaspoon salt
2   egg yolks, slightly beaten
2   egg whites
1½ cups buttermilk
6   tablespoons butter, melted

Preheat waffle baker. Mix all dry ingredients in a large mixing bowl. In another bowl mix yolks, buttermilk, and melted butter. Just before baking, stir the wet ingredients into the bowl of dry ingredients. Stir! Do not beat. Blend well, but briefly.

Now the extra step! With an electric beater, beat the egg whites until light and fluffy like a cloud or cotton candy, but not dry. This will not take long. Next fold egg whites into the batter, pulling up from the bottom of the bowl and blending into the dough.

Ladle batter onto baker to about an inch from edges. Do NOT lift cover during baking. Lift cover when time is up according to manufacturer's directions.

Use a fork to carefully lift and loosen baked waffles. Reheat the waffle baker before pouring the batter for the next waffle.

Notre Dame College Providence Hall Pancakes, Large Batch!

I was told that Sister Mary Anthon (now Sister Janet Kondrat) worked on this recipe. The pancakes were prepared for the Sisters who were studying, working, or teaching while living at Notre Dame College. These pancakes were the "best ever" I thought. Perhaps this large recipe will come in handy at a family reunion or a fundraiser for a church, school, or organization. Such a good recipe should not go to waste!

Serves 20 to 30 (2 large pancakes, 4 inches each).

9   cups flour
2   cups cornmeal
8   teaspoons baking powder
8   teaspoons sugar
1¾ teaspoons baking soda
1¾ tablespoons salt
8   eggs
½   gallon buttermilk
1 stick (½ cup) margarine, melted
Cooking oil or fat

In a 2 to 3-gallon mixing bowl mix all dry ingredients. In small saucepot melt the margarine. In another gallon-size bowl or pot, break eggs and beat until creamy. Add the buttermilk to the eggs and stir well.

When margarine cools, pour it into buttermilk/egg mixture. Add milk/egg/butter mixture to dry ingredients within a half hour of frying. The batter needs time to rise, or leaven.

Preheat griddle to 350°. Ladle cooking oil/fat onto griddle. After griddle is seasoned, you will need less. Ladle pancake batter per the size pancake desired. I suggest using a #16 dipper, which would yield about a 4-ounce pancake.

Look for bubbles to emerge around edges of pancake, and when you see bubbles in center, flip pancakes over. You will get into a rhythm. Pancakes will rise in center and when after a light tap "on the roof" they remain so, they are done. You will be able to determine doneness after a few pancakes. If you must, try one to be sure!

Note: If serving over an extended period of time, such as an all-morning pancake breakfast, refrigerate batter and take out small batches as needed for frying. Batter is potentially hazardous due to raw egg and moisture.

Pancakes, Small Batch (Very good!)
Provided by Sister Janet Kondrat

Serves 10 to12.

3¾	cups all-purpose flour
1	tablespoon baking powder
1	tablespoon white granulated sugar
1½	teaspoon baking soda
3	tablespoons shortening
1½	teaspoon salt
3	eggs
3	cups buttermilk

Follow frying directions in previous large batch recipe.

Mama Burke's Irish Soda Bread

From the mother of Sister Mary Brigid Burke (now Sister Mary Ann Burke)

4   cups flour
½   cup sugar
1   teaspoon baking powder
½   teaspoon baking soda
½   cup butter or oleo
2   cups seedless raisins
1½ cups buttermilk
1   egg
4   cups hot water (for soaking raisins)

Preheat the oven to 375°. Soak the raisins in hot water. In another bowl place flour, sugar, baking powder, baking soda, and stir to blend.

Add the solid butter (or oleo) in chunks and work in between your hands as you would to make pie dough. Use the light circular motion of sliding one hand against the other lightly so as not to melt the fat with the warmth of your hands. Do this until all fat is worked into dry mix and looks like dry pie dough. Drain the raisins and add to the dough.

In a small bowl, beat together the egg and buttermilk. Add buttermilk/egg mixture to dough and stir in until blended. Turn out on lightly floured surface and gently form a circular loaf.

Grease and flour a black 10-inch iron skillet and place loaf in it. Form a cross lightly over the center of loaf by pressing the edge of your palm into top of loaf.

Bake for 30 minutes. Then turn oven down to 350° and bake for 30 minutes more. Set skillet on top of stove and cool for 10 to 15 minutes. Then remove loaf to cooling rack or tabletop. When cool enough to slice, cut loaf in half lengthwise and then turn on end and slice in horseshoe shaped slices to serve. Nice with real butter!

Sliced Cheese

Assorted cheese slices were served on a platter to each table and accompanied by sliced Hough Bakery bread, hot cross buns, or other sweet rolls. Toasted bread was less frequent. It took longer to prepare for such large numbers of Sisters. If one dining room had toast, the other three dining rooms did not.

At first, eating cheese for breakfast, even with the jelly served with it, was a true penance for me. Eventually I came to enjoy it!

MEAT DISHES

Cold Cuts of Luncheon Meats

Here was a taste of Germany: Cold meat slices for
breakfast, often featuring hard salami. I could have used
a little cheese to help get this down early in the morning.

Cold cuts often appeared at breakfast on a second or
third class feast day. (Remember that bacon was "first
class"!) It was not unusual to have a fruit-filled Hough
Bakery Danish and a thin slice or two of hard salami to
start the day.

Pork Croquettes

This was a family favorite and part of "The Brown
Meal." The finished flavor should have a sage taste. You
may vary your spices depending on the pork. I find the
grocery store pork leaner than what the Sisters had
available. To compensate for loss of moisture, I added
some water to the pan.

You may like to test a very small sample by frying a
tiny patty ahead of time, tasting it before baking the
batch, and adding seasoning to your taste. Sister Thaddea
(now Sister Veronica Blasko) did this and often
exclaimed: "I would like more salt!"

Serves 10–12 (3 to 4-ounce servings).

1   pound ground pork
1   small clove garlic, fresh peeled
1   small, peeled yellow onion, quartered
1   teaspoon salt
1   teaspoon black pepper
1   teaspoon ground sage
1   12-ounce box of unseasoned breadcrumbs
½   cup water

Preheat oven to 400°.

Grind onion and garlic in blender until smooth. In a 4-quart mixing bowl, combine all ingredients except the breadcrumbs and mix them with your hands.

Place breadcrumbs in a pan.

Divide pork mixture into six even portions or scoops. You may wish to make portions smaller to yield more croquettes.

Roll portions in breadcrumbs, coating the pork completely. Form oval croquettes with your hands so they resemble little meatloaves. Lay them side by side in a 9 x 13-inch baking pan.

Place uncovered pan of croquettes in 400° oven for 45 to 50 minutes or until the croquettes are firm to the touch and crisp and golden on top.

Pour off any fat in the pan.

Serve hot. You may wish to make your favorite gravy or sauce.

Our croquettes were usually accompanied by sauerkraut, mashed potatoes, and applesauce.

Basic Meatloaf

This basic recipe may be adapted to your seasoning preferences. The Sisters sometimes added ketchup and mustard, Worcestershire sauce, and various herbs, including garlic. My personal preferences included those mentioned with perhaps some Italian herb blend.

The New Country Pie (the following recipe) could incorporate this basic meatloaf recipe and the topping of rice blended with cheese and tomato sauce.

Serves 8.

2   pounds lean ground beef
2   cups breadcrumbs
½   cup milk
½   cup chopped onion
2   eggs
1   teaspoon salt
½   teaspoon pepper
Water and ketchup or BBQ sauce (optional)

Mix all together in large mixing bowl, adding other ingredients as desired, such as minced garlic, herbs, ketchup, or mustard. Pour mixture into loaf pan and shape and pack lightly to form loaf.

To give loaf a glaze, sprinkle water over the top and baste with ketchup or BBQ sauce.

Bake in 350° oven for 1½ hours. Let stand 5 minutes and drain off drippings.

New Country Pie

This meat pie is similar to shepherd's pie, with a meatloaf crust or shell, topped with a cheesy rice filling. The flavors are Italian, and the look is a bit like pizza pie! It makes a great comfort food supper on a winter's evening. *Option:* Use the previous meatloaf recipe for the meat.

Serves 6 to 8.

1½ pound of ground sirloin
1   small yellow onion
2   tablespoons fresh curly parsley
1   teaspoon dried thyme
1   cup dried seasoned breadcrumbs (I prefer Italian.)
1/8 teaspoon salt
1/8 teaspoon black pepper
1   egg
1   cup of milk
8   ounces grated cheddar cheese
2   cups long grain white rice
4   cups water
2   cups Italian sauce (I prefer Dei Fratelli.)

Combine meat, onion, parsley, thyme, breadcrumbs, salt, pepper. Press mixture into two 9-inch deep dish pie tins or Pyrex dishes, as you would a pie crust. Bake meat about ½ hour at 400° until firm but not dry. Drain off fat.

Add rice to water and cover with lid. Cook over low fire for about 20 minutes until tender. Mix rice with your favorite Italian sauce. Toss grated cheese into the tomato rice mix. Save some to spread over the top later.

Spread this mixture over the pre-cooked meat. Cover with foil and bake in a 375° oven for about 20 minutes. Remove the cover and add remaining cheese. Bake another 5 to 10 minutes to melt cheese. Remove from oven and let set 5 to 10 minutes. Cut pie into portion size and serve hot. Delicious!

Beef Porcupines

Porcupines were regular dinner fare. They reminded me of stuffed cabbage rolls without the cabbage.

Serves 8.

2   pounds lean ground beef
1   cup uncooked white rice
¼   cup grated onion
1   teaspoon salt
½   teaspoon black pepper
2½ cups condensed tomato soup
2   cups hot water

Mix ground beef, rice, salt, pepper, and onions. Shape into oval loaves and place side by side in 8 ½ x 11-inch baking pan or similar casserole. Dilute the tomato soup with 2 cups of hot water and pour this over the croquettes.

Bake covered at 350° for 45 minutes to 1 hour. Check in between. Loaves are done if rice is poking out of them. Sauce will be partly absorbed.

Meat Pinwheels

I always understood this to be another German heritage food or a Depression era attempt to enhance leftovers. However, I thought it usually very tasty.

Serves 8 to 12.

2   cups flour
3   teaspoons baking powder
1   teaspoon salt
¼   teaspoon soda
¼   cup shortening
¾   cup buttermilk or sour milk

Work the shortening into flour as for pie dough until like little pebbles. Add milk, stirring in gently. (Biscuits must not be over handled. Use a light touch!) Knead gently on lightly flour-dusted surface about 20 to 30 seconds. Roll out lightly with rolling pin to a rectangle shape about 1¼ inch thick and 12 x 4 to 6 inches.

Filling: We used chopped leftover beef stew with a little gravy. Sometimes we added other meats—like a wet hash! Be creative! Tuna, minced ham, or salmon would be tasty alternatives to the beef. Other options are a BBQ chopped pork and light sauce, or even a thick ground beef spaghetti sauce. You can also add grated cheese.

Spread filling over dough and then roll as for jelly roll. Cut with sharp knife or scissors into ½ inch slices. Cradle slice in hand and place on greased cookie sheet. Bake at 375 ° for 25 to 30 minutes.

We served the beef pinwheels hot with a hot apple-raisin sauce with a dash of cloves or allspice as an accompaniment passed like gravy at table. Sometimes we just had meat gravy.

Suggestion: Use Bisquick to make pinwheel dough.

Dorothy Dear's Chicken Casserole

Serves about 12.

4   cups diced cooked chicken
2½ cups diced celery
2   tablespoons diced onion
2   10 3/4-ounce cans cream of chicken soup
4   cups cooked rice
2   cups mayonnaise
4   tablespoons melted butter
1½ cups corn flake crumbs
Almonds, sliced (optional)

Mix first six ingredients and place in shallow pan. Mix melted butter and corn flake crumbs. Sprinkle over chicken and rice mixture. Optional: Spread sliced almonds over this. Bake for 40 minutes at 350°.

MEATLESS ENTRÉES

Sister Dorotheus's Cottage Cheese and Noodle Casserole

Serves about 20.

5   pounds cottage cheese
2   pounds medium egg noodles
8   eggs, beaten
1   medium onion, sautéed
1   cup celery, diced small
Black pepper, to taste
Corn flake crumbs (1 pound box)
Cooking oil

Cook and drain noodles. Sauté onions and celery. In a 2-gallon bowl mix cottage cheese, noodles, and sautéed vegetables. Add beaten eggs and black pepper and mix well. Pour into oiled chafing pan 13 x 20 x 2 inches. Top with corn flake crumbs. Bake at 325° for 1 hour.

Swedish Eggs

This dish was prepared on Fridays or during Lent usually for supper. I remember it accompanied by hot spinach and fried potatoes! Count on two eggs per portion.

Serves 3.

1 pound American or cheddar cheese grated (medium shred)
6 large eggs
¾ cup milk
2 tablespoons oil or shortening for greasing baking dish
Salt, pepper, or herbs

Grease the bottom and sides of a 4 x 4-inch baking pan or similar casserole dish with oil or shortening. Grate cheese into baking dish and make six nests by scooping out a hole in the bed of cheese, mounding the cheese up and around edges of nest hole.

Drop cracked eggs into nest holes. With a spoon, moisten cheese around each egg nest with dribbles of milk (about 1 tablespoon per nest). Bake at 300° for 10 to 15 minutes or until set. Egg yolk should be cooked but not rubbery. White will be set. Serve while very warm.

Sweet Potatoes and Cottage Cheese

These make a delicious Lenten entrée.

Servings will vary.

Sweet potatoes, medium size
Cottage cheese

Bake unpeeled sweet potatoes at 450° for one hour or until fork tender. Cut them in half. Serve them with a scoop of cold cottage cheese as a side or as topping.

Sweet Rice and Cheese Slices

This meal was a favorite of the community, probably because of the sweet rice—so creamy, warm, and delicately flavored with cinnamon. Using the cinnamon stick preserved the white look and avoided a dusty brown color that cinnamon powder would cause.

Serves 6.

1   cup white, short grain white rice
2   cups milk, 2% or whole
1   small stick of cinnamon
¼   cup white granulated sugar
1   pinch of salt
Water
Cheese

Fill the lower pot of a 2-quart double boiler with enough water to touch the bottom of the top pot. Pour the milk in the top pot and then add the rice.

Cook uncovered on low heat for about 45 minutes, stirring occasionally. You may have to add milk depending on evaporation. Rice will be tender when done, and most milk absorbed.

Serve with assorted slices of cheese.

Cheese-Rice Croquettes

Some would say, "This recipe is a lot of work!" I would answer: "Oh! But it is so worth it!" Once you have made a batch, it goes faster! The Sisters looked forward to cheese-rice croquettes in Lent and on Fridays during the year.

Serves 12.

2   cups white long grain rice
4   cups water
1   teaspoon salt
1   tablespoon Worcestershire sauce
½   pound American cheese (shredded)
1   tablespoon mustard
2   eggs
1   cup milk
2   cups unseasoned breadcrumbs
1-2 quarts frying oil (peanut oil or melted Crisco)
Fruit preserves

Cook rice in 4 cups of salted water in an uncovered 2-quart pot on top of stove until water is absorbed. This will take about 15 minutes.

Drain hot, cooked rice and immediately pour it into a 2-gallon mixing bowl. Add Worcestershire sauce, mustard, and shredded cheese and mix well. Set aside.

Pour breadcrumbs into 9 x 13-inch baking dish. In a 2-quart bowl, beat the eggs and milk for the custard. Using a #10 size scoop or a large spoon, scoop rice to make croquettes of about ½ cup each. Drop each croquette into the custard, and then lift it out with a slotted spoon or spatula, allowing excess custard to drain. Drop wet croquette into breadcrumbs. With your hands, toss croquette lightly to coat all sides. Shape with hands into a circular patty. Place the croquettes on a baking sheet to set.

In an iron skillet or French fryer, heat about a quart of cooking oil to 375°. (Peanut oil is good for deep frying as it has a high smoke point, meaning it tolerates high temperatures.) Using a slotted metal spoon or metal spatula to keep croquettes in oil, fry them until golden. (About 2 to 3 minutes.)

Set croquettes on a baking sheet. Prior to serving, place sheet of croquettes in a 350° oven for about 15 minutes.

Before plating, make an indentation in center of croquettes with a teaspoon. Fill each one with a tablespoon of your favorite fruit preserves. (Blackberry and strawberry preserves are especially flavorful and colorful.) Serve hot at once!

What Is Proofing?

Proofing yeast is testing the yeast to insure that it is active. The first step is placing the yeast in a bowl, moistening it with water, and adding sugar to feed it. Then the hydrated yeast is covered with a kitchen towel or placed it an off oven to retain its warmth and moisture. In about 15 minutes, the yeast should "prove" to be alive by foaming into a light brown cloud. The key to baking with yeast is temperature control. Use a thermometer and follow the instructions that come with your yeast.

Proofing dough refers to the rising of dough through the action of yeast. The yeast reacts to ingredients added to it, resulting in fermentation. Carbon dioxide is released and the dough rises. Proofing occurs in a warm, humid place. I put my dough in my off gas oven, uncovered, and place a small bowl of water on the floor of the oven. A recipe may call for two proofings.

Shamrock Potato Rolls

This recipe was a favorite for special feast days. I think Sister Mary Brigid had something to do with the shamrock form. The dough can also be used to make rolls or loaves of various shapes.

Serves about 24.

1   tablespoon instant dry yeast
½ cup warm water (112°-115°)
½ cup mashed potato, newly cooked or leftover
½ cup shortening or butter
½ cup sugar
¾ teaspoon salt
1   cup milk, scalded
1   egg
4-5 cups all-purpose flour
Butter
Cooking oil

Combine yeast, warm water, and 1 teaspoon sugar and let proof about 15 minutes. In a one-quart or medium size pot, heat milk to a warm temperature. Add potato, shortening, sugar, and salt. When still warm but not hot, add the yeast mixture.

Beat the egg with a small amount of milk and stir into warm yeast mixture. Mix well.

Pour this mixture into large mixing bowl with dough hook attachment or other 2 to 3- gallon bowl if kneading by hand. Stir the flour into the wet mixture until dough is smooth and elastic and comes away from sides of the bowl. Add a little more flour if dough still sticks to sides of the bowl.

Add a little oil to sides of a large bowl. Set the dough in it and then turn the dough over so it is oiled side up.

Place uncovered dough in an off oven with a small bowl of water on the floor of the oven. Plan on an hour for dough to double. To test it, poke finger into dough. If the hole does not immediately fill in, dough is ready.

Punch dough down, divide it in half and place halves on flour-dusted surface. Cut each half into 12 portions. Work quickly because dough is growing.

Divide each portion into 3 lumps and roll each lump to form a ball. Place the 3 lumps side by side in a greased muffin pan compartment, forming a shamrock.

Let rolls rise to double in a warm area (may use an off oven). When rolls are doubled, bake in preheated 375° oven for 20 to 25 minutes until rolls are golden.

Remove the rolls and brush them with butter. Loosen rolls from sides and bottoms of muffin pan with a butter knife so they don't sweat.

When rolls are cool, remove from pan, cover with plastic wrap or foil or place in plastic bags to retain moisture. Store at room temperature. If kept more than a day or two, store in refrigerator or freeze in plastic bags.

Kneading Dough

To knead by hand, turn dough out onto a floured table surface with the help of a baker's scraper. Pull dough from the top to the center of and press down with the heels of your hands. Turn the dough slightly. Then pull dough down again. Repeat this circular kneading motion for 5 to 7 minutes or until dough is smooth and elastic. Add flour if necessary.

Refrigerator Sweet Cinnamon Rolls

This recipe was often used to make sweet rolls for a Sunday or feast day breakfast. The rolls might be made into pinwheels or just braided and frosted. Sometimes raisins would be added to the dough or a topping of ground nuts splashed onto the frosted topping.

Note: This bread dough recipe can be prepared ahead of time, placed in a large oiled bowl or pot, covered tightly to retain moisture, and refrigerated for 1 to 3 days prior to use. Dough should be taken from refrigerator about 2 to 3 hours prior to working the dough. Time may vary depending on room conditions. Dough will warm up and double. After dough doubles in volume, punch down and shape.

Serves 16 to 18.

¾ cup milk, whole
½ cup sugar
2 teaspoons salt
½ cup butter
½ cup warm water (110°-115°)
2 tablespoons instant dried yeast *
2 eggs
4-5 cups flour (We used all-purpose flour.)
Shortening

* More yeast is used in refrigerator dough than in previous recipe to compensate for the slowed yeast growth caused by low temperatures.

Filling:
¼ pound butter
1 cup dark or light brown sugar
3 teaspoons cinnamon
8 ounces raisins

Glaze:
2 pounds powdered sugar
½ cup white corn syrup
¾ cup warm water
2 teaspoons vanilla
Flavorings like almond, chocolate or maple (optional)

Proof the yeast by dissolving it in warm water and adding
½ teaspoon sugar. After about 15 minutes, the yeast
should form a brown foamy cloud.

In a 1-quart saucepan, heat 1 cup milk until bubbly
(about 120°). Add sugar, salt, and butter. Cool milk
mixture to lukewarm (about 115°). In a small bowl, beat
2 eggs. Stir in a cup of warm milk mixture little by little
to moderate the temperatures. Introduce this egg mixture
into the warm milk mixture in the saucepan. Then stir in
the yeast.

Pour mixture into a 1-gallon mixing bowl with a
dough hook attachment or for hand-mixing use a 2-gallon
stainless steel bowl and wooden spoon. Mix, gradually
adding flour. Beat until dough is smooth and comes away
from the sides of the bowl. If it still sticks to the sides,
add a wee bit more flour.

Turn dough out onto floured surface and knead 5 to 7
minutes in a circular fashion. Set dough into oiled bowl,
and flip dough oiled side up. Cover with lid and place in
refrigerator for at least 3 hours (and up to 3 days).

Grease a 9 x 13-inch baking pan and a 9-inch pie pan. Mix brown sugar with raisins and cinnamon and melt the butter. Roll dough into a rectangle. Brush with some of the melted butter. Sprinkle sugar mixture over rectangle. Roll up dough away from you, tightly pinching edges at the ends together as you roll. With a sharp butcher knife, cut pinwheel circles about ¼ inch thick and lay these sliced side down on pans. Let pinwheels raise to double. Then bake at 375° for 15 to 20 minutes or until golden. Remove from oven and brush warm rolls with leftover butter.

When rolls are cool, mix the ingredients for the glaze and frost them.

Jason Sotkovski's Two Too-Easy Pizzas

Back home in Warren and Niles, Ohio, in the 50s and 60s there were many Italians, and pizza shops abounded! Sadly, convent pizza bore little resemblance to authentic Italian pizza. The convent dough was sweet, and worse, the toppings were ground beef and American cheese! We rarely tasted even this pizza—after all, German heritage predominated in our food customs. Consequently, when we arrived in the dining room, starving from the afternoon's hard work, and found that the menu included pizza, despite the imperfections, we did enjoy it!

Jason, a chef at Holly Hill Nursing Home, developed this little specialty pizza dough and shared his recipe for this book. Easy to make and to remember.

I make one white pizza and one with red sauce.

2   cups hot water (115°)
2   teaspoons Red Star instant dry yeast (4-ounce bottle)
2   teaspoons sugar
2   teaspoons olive oil
2-4 cups high protein bread flour (I used King Arthur.)
2   teaspoons salt
Corn meal to sprinkle on stones
2   15-inch pizza stones (or cookie sheets or round
baking pans)

Preheat a 2-quart mixing bowl with very hot water, then
empty out. Add 2 cups hot water to bowl. Dissolve 2
teaspoons yeast and 2 teaspoons sugar in it. Put in an off
oven with a dish of water on its floor. Or place yeast in a
warm spot and cover with a kitchen towel. Allow about
15 minutes to proof. Should form a brown, frothy cloud.
    Add 2 teaspoons oil to the yeast. Add 2 teaspoons of
salt to flour, then add flour mixture to wet ingredients,
stirring in with wooden spoon. Use a plastic baker's
scraper to turn out dough onto lightly floured table. Work
dough with hands, forming a soft ball. Knead dough,
adding only enough flour to form a soft dough and
prevent sticking to your fingers. Knead for 5 to 7 minutes
or until dough is smooth and elastic. Turn dough into
oiled bowl, turning oiled side up.
    Place bowl of dough in an off oven, uncovered, to
raise to double (about 1 hour). Place a dish of warm
water on floor of oven to add humidity for the rising
dough. Once dough has doubled, punch down and divide
in half. Sprinkle corn meal on the two 15-inch pizza
stones (or cookie sheets or baking pans). Place lump of
dough on each, press and coax dough into circular shape,
adding tablespoon of olive oil to surface of each pie to

ease the stretching. Let pies raise for about ½ hour in warm area.

Bake at 425° for about 20 minutes. Remove from oven when cheese is melted and dough is golden. Cool.

(Jason suggests par baking the crust for about 10 minutes at 425° to seal the surface and prevent a soggy dough. Then add toppings and bake.)

Toppings:

White Pizza
2   tablespoons olive oil
2   tablespoons fresh grated garlic
½   cup parmesan/Romano dry cheese
1   tablespoon dried oregano
1   tablespoon of dried basil (or torn fresh basil, enough to dot the pie)
1   cup fresh green pepper slices
1   cup fresh mushroom slices
1   cup sliced sweet onion
2   ounces sliced pepperoni or 2 cups sliced, cooked Italian sausage
4   ounces fresh mozzarella, grated (about 2 cups)

Mix the olive oil and garlic and spread over pizza dough. Add the toppings, sprinkling cheese over all last.

Red Pizza
2 cups sauce (prepared pizza sauce or your own made from a 29-ounce can thick puree.)

Add the dry spices and parmesan cheese to sauce and spread sauce over dough. Spread the other toppings over pizza, finishing with mozzarella.

SOUP AND SALADS

Buttermilk Soup

Serves 3.

2   cups cold buttermilk (whole milk version)
2-3 tablespoons white granulated sugar (more or less to
     taste
½   teaspoon cinnamon
Dash of nutmeg
Pinch of salt
Cubes of cake, broken cookies, or Stella Doro Anisette
Toast

In order to set flavors, prepare about an hour before
serving. First mix cinnamon, nutmeg, and salt into sugar
and stir. Add sugar mixture into very cold buttermilk. To
serve, top the serving bowl with cake cubes or broken
cookies. For a delicious topping, break Stella Doro
Anisette Toast into chunks.

Waldorf Salad

Serves 4 to 6.

1   cup mayonnaise (I prefer Hellman's.)
¼   cup lemon juice
1   pound (3 cups) McIntosh apples (or any red-skinned
     apples)

2　cups celery, thinly sliced
1　cup English walnuts, chopped or broken (not too fine)
1　cup dark seedless raisins
Lettuce

In medium bowl mix mayonnaise and lemon juice with spoon. Slice unpeeled apples and remove core, then dice into small cubes. Add apples to mayo mix and stir. Add celery, walnuts, and raisins and stir. Serve on a bed of lettuce.

Cranberry Sour Cream Salad

Serves 6.

1　3-ounce package of cherry jello
1　cup boiling water
1　16-ounce can of whole cranberry sauce
½　cup chopped celery
¼　cup chopped walnuts
1　cup sour cream
Water
Lettuce
Mayonnaise

Combine jello powder with hot water. When it is dissolved, add the cranberry sauce. Pour into jello mold and let stand to gel. Mix celery, walnuts, sour cream together. When jello is almost hard, stir this mixture into it. Serve on lettuce leaf with mayonnaise.

Cottage Cheese Summer Salad

I used this recipe in the summer in Middleburg, Virginia, for Notre Dame Sisters on retreat or studying at the Middleburg Institute. It is easy to adapt for larger numbers. Jello is added for color and taste and to complement summer fruits. For cantaloupe we chose orange jello, for strawberries red jello, and so on.

Serves 6 to 8.

1   pound cream style cottage cheese
1   3-ounce package of jello, any flavor
1   15-ounce can mandarin oranges
1   15-ounce can pineapple chunks
1   8-ounce carton Cool Whip
Orange slices
Lettuce

Mix cottage cheese and dry jello powder. Add Cool Whip and the mandarin oranges and pineapple chunks or substitute summer fruit such as honeydew melon, cantaloupe, strawberries, and peaches. Garnish with orange slices. Serve on a bed of lettuce.

Authentic Hot German Potato Salad

I recently discovered this version of a German favorite, provided by Christa Hearn, Karen Mansi's sister-in-law, who is from Germany. This unique recipe is minus the bacon fat, fried onion, and cider vinegar in the Notre Dame recipe and makes a potato salad that is delicious and perhaps healthier! The sweet and sour flavors and the bacon combine for the same familiar flavor. I include it here for another taste of Germany.

Serves 12.

8   cups sliced raw Russet potatoes (about 3 pounds)
½   teaspoon salt in water
4   teaspoons pickle juice from Hengstenberg Gherkin pickles
1   cup cooked bacon, crumbled or diced (about ¾ pound raw bacon)
1   cup large yellow onion, diced (½ cup to be cooked with potato and other ½ used for sauce)
½   cup rice vinegar
6   tablespoons mayonnaise (I use Hellman's.)
¼   teaspoon nutmeg
¼   teaspoon dried dill

Peel and slice potatoes about ¼ inch thick. Cook covered, on medium heat, in two-quart pot of salted water. Cook until tender but firm (about 10 to15 minutes).

Drain off water. Water may be saved and used for soup.

Pour potatoes into 9 x 13-inch baking dish. Sprinkle crumbled bacon over potatoes.

In 1-quart bowl mix pickle juice, mayonnaise, diced raw onion, rice vinegar, nutmeg and dill. Pour sauce over warm sliced potatoes in casserole dish and toss lightly.

Serve warm or cold. Nice with hot dogs or a bologna sandwich!

Wilted Salad with Hot Bacon Dressing

Serves about 6.

1	pound (large bunch) of greens (escarole, endive, dandelion greens, or Bibb lettuce)
4	slices bacon, fried, drained and crumbled
4	tablespoons of bacon fat
2	tablespoons flour
2	tablespoons cider vinegar or red wine vinegar
2	tablespoons white granulated sugar
½	cup raw Spanish onion, diced
1	teaspoon salt
½	teaspoon black pepper
½	cup water

Trim ends and dark, tough, or damaged leaves. Cut bunch into half-inch slices. Place cut lettuce in cold water in a sink or bowl. Toss lettuce in water thoroughly to loosen any soil, then transfer lettuce to a colander to drain off water. Place well drained greens in mixing bowl.

In large skillet sauté bacon until crisp. Remove bacon strips and drain them on paper towel. Drain fat from fry pan. Return 4 tablespoons of fat to pan and sauté onion in it. Add 2 tablespoons flour and stir. Then add 2 tablespoons vinegar, 2 tablespoons sugar, salt, and pepper. Stir to blend into a nice hot gravy or dressing. Add ½ cup water, and thin as desired with more water.

Just prior to serving, pour hot dressing over salad and lightly toss. Crumble bacon and add it. Serve soon, for the longer the salad sets, the more the greens shrink.

POTATO RECIPES

One cannot say enough about the central role of potato in German cuisine, and this was reflected in the numerous ways Sisters were served this "apple of the earth."

Au Gratin Potatoes with French Onion Dip

Dean Dairy made donations to the Sisters for a time. The Notre Dame workmen would pick up the donation in a truck and return with a variety of products. One was French onion dip, which went very well with potatoes. A similar product is used in this recipe.

Serves 10 to 12.

6-8 medium Idaho potatoes, peeled, sliced thin
1   pound Wisconsin white cheddar cheese, grated
1   pound Helluvagood French onion dip
2   cups milk
Black pepper, to taste

Preheat oven to 300°.
Boil and drain potatoes. Place them in an oiled 9 x 13-inch pan or casserole. Spread onion dip over potatoes. Sprinkle shredded cheddar over all. Pour milk over casserole. Sprinkle with black pepper. Cover casserole lightly with foil and bake potatoes for about ½ hour. Uncover and bake until golden, about 15 more minutes. Add milk if needed to keep moist. Serve hot.

Potato Patties

The Sisters loved these! Sister Dorotheus often planned for patties when we had any leftover potatoes that could be mashed and formed into patties, even sweet potatoes! I remember Sister instructing us to add "just a little nutmeg"!

An elderly gentleman I encountered told me of his Swedish heritage food customs that included a delicious nutmeg flavored potato patty. There it is, that Swedish influence from Northern Germany! This was confirmed when I found a recipe for potato patties in the cookbook *Spoonfuls of Germany* by Nadia Hasani.

2   pounds yellow potatoes (Russet or Yukon Gold)
2   tablespoons unsalted butter
2   tablespoons milk
1   pinch of ground nutmeg (or ½ teaspoon more)
1   egg
2   tablespoons all-purpose flour
Vegetable oil for sautéing
Salt to taste

In a 2-quart pot, cover potatoes with water. Add a dash of salt and cook until tender. Drain off water and mash the potatoes. Heat milk and butter together in small saucepan or microwave and add to potatoes. Add nutmeg. Stir. Then add egg and flour and knead to form a soft dough.

Heat oil in a large skillet. With hands moistened with cold water, shape mixture into 3-inch patties. Drop patties into skillet. Brown one side and carefully flip to other side to brown. Serve hot with a side of applesauce.

Parsleyed Potatoes

1 serving per 4 ½ -ounce potato.

Potatoes (new, Yukon or Idaho that keep their shape)
Salt
Butter
Fresh parsley, chopped fine
Water

Peel potatoes (unless they are thin-skinned). Cut in cubes or thick slices. Set in pot, cover with water, and add a dash of salt. Cover pot and cook on low heat until tender, 15 to 20 minutes. Drain off water. Melt butter. Dribble it over potatoes and toss lightly. Right before serving, sprinkle parsley over potatoes and toss them.

O'Brien Potatoes

I always liked these because of the name. My paternal grandmother was an O'Brien! The green peppers are the O'Brien part.

1 serving per 4 ½ -ounce potato.

Potatoes
Hot oil or bacon fat
Onions
Green peppers

Cube potatoes and slice onions and green peppers. Cook all ingredients in hot oil or bacon fat.

Hoppelpoppel

Hoppelpoppel is an old German "peasant dish." We enjoyed this potato dish at home. My grandfather, Lawrence Lonsway, put on his cook apron to prepare this dish, according to my mother, Dorothy Quinn. He had the idea that Grandma Sadie, my very German grandmother, might appreciate a respite from cooking on a Sunday morning. She did! Mom loved that memory, and we loved the potatoes!

Serves 8.

2   pounds potatoes (suggest Idaho)
1   small Spanish onion, sliced thin
1   small green or red pepper, sliced in slivers
1½ pounds bacon
8   medium eggs
Bacon fat

Fry and drain bacon. Slice potatoes 1/8 inch thick or cut into ¼ inch cues. Boil potatoes in salt water 5 to 10 minutes until slightly tender. Don't overcook. Drain potatoes.

Sauté onion and pepper in bacon drippings until tender. Add potatoes and bacon. Cook until browned.

Beat eggs and pour over all in pan. Cover pan and cook 5 to 10 minutes until eggs set.

Garnish as you wish. Tomato slices are nice.

Fried Potatoes

A friend states that her German sister-in-law announced: "Most German dishes start with a little bacon and onion!" That is how fried potatoes are prepared.

Serves 8.

8   medium potatoes (Idaho potatoes are good.)
1   large yellow onion
Bacon fat
Salt and pepper to taste

Slice potatoes to thinness desired. Heat pan of bacon fat and add generous slices of onion. Add potatoes. Brown on one side and toss. Add salt and pepper to taste and cover until all is tender. Enjoy the aroma! Serve hot with ketchup or vinegar.

DESSERTS

For jubilee celebrations, profession of vows, and investment there would be many guests. The refrigerator cookie was a great way to work ahead to meet demands.

Refrigerator Chocolate Pinwheel Cookies

Makes 4 dozen.

½ cup shortening
½ cup sugar
1 egg yolk
1½ teaspoon vanilla
½ cup flour
½ teaspoon salt
½ teaspoon baking powder
3 tablespoons milk
1 1-ounce square unsweetened chocolate, melted

Cream sugar, shortening, egg yolk, vanilla. Add sifted dry ingredients alternately with the milk. Divide dough in half. Mix chocolate into one half. Roll each half 1/8 inch thick on wax paper.

Place the white part onto the chocolate so that the chocolate part extends ½ inch further on the edge toward which you roll. Roll as for jelly roll. Wrap in wax paper and chill thoroughly.

Slice thin and place on ungreased cookie sheet. Bake in 375° oven about 10 minutes.

Refrigerator Date/Walnut Pinwheel Cookies

Makes 6 dozen.

4   cups flour
1   teaspoon baking soda
1   teaspoon cream of tartar
1   cup butter
2   eggs
2   cups brown sugar
1   teaspoon vanilla
1½ cups chopped English walnuts
1   pound whole pitted dates
Water

Mix together flour, baking soda, and cream of tartar. Cream butter, eggs, and brown sugar in mixing bowl. Add flour mixture, vanilla, and nuts. Mix well. Shape dough into two rolls and chill for an hour or longer in refrigerator.

Chop dates into small pieces and place in small saucepan. Add ¾ to 1 cup water. Cook over low heat, stirring until dates become a chunky sauce. Remove from heat and cool. Add chopped English walnuts to dates.

One roll at a time, place on lightly floured table and roll into a horizontal rectangle about 12 x 4 inches. Spread on sauce. Roll up dough from side nearest you. Roll forward, tightly forming a log. Slice in 1/8-inch disks and lay them on cookie sheet about ¼ inch apart. Bake at 375° for about 10 minutes until set and lightly browned. Remove to cool and loosen with spatula.

Store in covered container to keep fresh.

Spice Refrigerator Cookies

Makes 8 dozen.

1   pound margarine
1   cup granulated sugar
1   cup brown sugar
4   eggs
5½ cups flour
1   teaspoon baking soda
2   teaspoon salt
2   teaspoons cinnamon
1   teaspoon ginger
½   teaspoon cloves

Cream sugars and margarine. Add eggs and mix. Mix together flour and spices. Add dry ingredients to wet ingredients and mix well. Form long logs of dough on lightly floured table. Place on wax paper and wrap up rolls. Refrigerate thoroughly and store until ready to bake. May store for a couple of days.

Slice about 1/8 inch thin. Place on ungreased cookie sheet. Bake at 375° for 7 minutes or until lightly browned.

Sister Amata's Orange Sugar Cookies

Makes 8 dozen.

1   pound (2 cups) margarine or butter
3   cups sugar
3   eggs

1/3   cup orange juice
1   orange for grated rind
6   cups flour
1   teaspoon baking soda

In mixing bowl, cream sugar and shortening. Add eggs, juice, orange rind, flour and refrigerate. Work with a small portion at a time. Roll about 1/8 inch thick and cut into desired shapes. Place on greased cookie sheet. Bake at 375° for 10 minutes.

Options: Beat egg and water and brush over cookies before baking. Or frost with icing when cookies cool.

Guess Again Cookies

Makes 4 to 5 dozen.

1   cup butter
2   cups flour
½   cup sugar plus some for topping
½   cup crushed potato chips
1   teaspoon vanilla
½   cup chopped pecans

Cream butter, sugar, and vanilla. Add potato chips and pecans. Gradually stir in flour. Roll dough into balls and place on ungreased baking sheet. Flatten with a fork and sprinkle top with sugar. Bake in 350° oven for 10 or 11 minutes.

Prune Kolache

In Slavic Village I learned about Eastern Europe pastries.

Makes about 3 dozen.

1 tablespoon dry yeast
½ cup cream, heated to very warm (100°)
½ cup sugar
¾ pound butter
3½ cups flour
½ teaspoon salt
4 egg yolks, slightly beaten

Filling:
Dried prunes
Sugar to taste
Cinnamon
Lemon zest or orange juice
(Alternate fillings: prune paste, fruit preserves, or dried fruit)

Prepare filling by soaking prunes in water for a few hours. Cook on low about 15 minutes, adding other ingredients. Mash with potato masher to make a puree.
    Dissolve yeast in warmed cream with sugar and let stand for about 10 minutes. Add salt to flour. Cut in butter into flour mixture as for piecrust. Add yeast mix and yolks to form soft dough. Cover tightly and let rise in warm place for 1 hour. Turn out on lightly floured table and roll out to about ½ inch thick. Cut circles in dough with round biscuit cutter or upside down glass. Make wide indentations in center of circles with thumb. Set filling on each. Let rise 15 minutes. Bake in 400° oven 15

to 20 minutes. Pastries will be firm and slightly golden.

Glaze (optional):
1½ cup powdered sugar
¼   cup water
¼   teaspoon real vanilla
dash of salt

Mix well until smooth. When pastries are cool, drizzle glaze back and forth to form white streaks.

Spicy Gingerbread

Gingerbread was a winter dessert. To retain moisture, do not over bake. It is better to anticipate less bake time.

Serves 9.

2½ cups all-purpose flour
½   cup molasses
½   cup sugar
½   cup shortening
1   egg
1½ teaspoon baking soda
1   teaspoon ground cinnamon
1   teaspoon ground ginger
½   teaspoon ground cloves
1   cup boiling water
Topping: whipped cream, applesauce, custard or lemon sauce (optional)

Preheat oven to 350°. Grease a 9-inch square baking pan and sprinkle with flour. In a large bowl with mixer on low speed, mix all ingredients. Beat on medium speed 3 minutes. Pour dough into pan. Bake 45 minutes or until toothpick inserted comes out clean. Cool pan on wire rack. Cut into nine servings and top with whipped cream or other complementary sauces.

Feast of St. Nicholas

The Sisters celebrated the feast of St. Nicholas on December 6 with gifts, games, and goodies. The holy bishop himself might appear accompanied by Ruprecht clothed in black and carrying twigs to punish the bad. This traditional celebration was inherited from the early German Sisters. I was delighted to be introduced to such tasty St. Nick customs as gingerbread men and apple dumplings.

Gingerbread Men Cookies

On the feast of St. Nicholas, every Sister received a gingerbread cookie at her place in keeping with the German custom. Usually these were in the shape of a bishop with a miter.

Makes 4 dozen.

½ cup molasses
½ cup white granulated sugar
½ cup shortening (1 stick margarine)
1 egg
3½ cups all-purpose flour
½ teaspoon baking soda
1 teaspoon ground ginger
Dash of salt

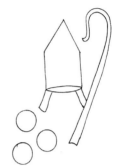

Frosting:
1¼ cup powdered sugar
¼ teaspoon cream of tartar
1 egg white
Food dye

Combine molasses and sugar in saucepan and boil 1 minute, then cool. Place shortening and molasses in mixing bowl and beat on medium speed. Add eggs and mix well. Combine flour, salt, baking soda, and ginger. Add dry ingredients to molasses mixture. Mix on low speed until well blended.

Form dough into 2 logs about 2 inches in diameter. Wrap in wax paper and refrigerate about 2 hours. On a lightly floured table, roll dough out to 1/8-inch thick. Cut dough into gingerbread men or other shapes and place on greased cookie sheet. Bake at 375° for 8 to 10 minutes.

In a small bowl sift powdered sugar and cream of tartar through fine sieve. Add egg white. Beat at high speed until stiff. On humid days, you may need more sugar. Add food coloring as desired. Fill paper cone or cake decorating envelope. Outline arms and feet and add decorations to each cookie.

Baked Apple Dumplings

Apple dumplings were a favorite dessert for the feast of St. Nicholas and one that everyone anticipated as the day drew near!

Serves 6.

2   cups all-purpose flour
1   teaspoon salt
2/3 cup shortening, like pork lard
5-6 tablespoons cold milk
6   medium baking apples, peeled and cored
½   cup white, granulated sugar
½   cup brown sugar, packed
½   teaspoon cinnamon
1   stick of butter

Sauce:
½   cup sugar
½   cup boiling water
1   teaspoon flour
1   pinch of cinnamon
1   pinch of salt
1   tablespoon butter (optional)

Sift flour and salt together in a large bowl. Cut shortening into flour with pastry blender or combine with hands until mixture is crumbly. Make a well in the center of the dough. Add milk in well and mix. Form 6 balls and roll into circles on lightly floured table.

Place an apple in the center of each circle. Mix brown sugar and cinnamon and sprinkle mixture into the core of each apple. Add a tablespoon of butter to center of each apple. Bring the dough up and around each one. Wet dough edges to seal and pinch closed. Turn each dumpling over and make 3 slashes on the bottom. Place apples right side up in 9 x 13-inch baking pan.

Make sauce by mixing sugar cinnamon, flour, and salt in saucepan on stove. (May add 1 tablespoon of butter for flavor and sheen.) Stir in water and cook for 2 to 3 minutes. Add sauce around apples.

Prick dumplings with fork to prevent bursting. Bake for ½ hour at 350°. Baste with sauce in bottom of pan. Bake another 15 minutes and baste again. Apples should be done and fork tender. Serve hot with additional sauce.

Bread Pudding

Serves about 12.

2   cups milk
2   eggs slightly beaten
½   cup sugar
1   teaspoon cinnamon or nutmeg
¼   teaspoon salt
6   cups soft bread cubes (or leftover cakes or cookies)
½   cup raisins

Mix milk, eggs, sugar, and spices to make custard. Add raisins to bread/cake cubes and place in a 9 x 13-inch baking pan. Pour custard over all. Let soak for a half hour. Bake uncovered in a 350° oven for 40 to 45 minutes.

Butterscotch Apples

Here was a dish that stood out in flavor. My first
experience of this apple dessert left me wanting to know
how it was made. My wish was granted, albeit on a large
scale.

The Sisters loved this apple specialty, and I sure do
too, enough to make these many years later. The results?
Just as pleasing as ever. (But on a smaller scale!)

Serves 6 to 8.

6   cups semi-tart cooking apples (6-8 medium apples)
(Melrose keep their shape and retain tartness.)
3   cups water
½   cup white granulated sugar
¼   cup unsalted, sweet butter
½   cup light brown sugar

Sauce:
3   tablespoons cornstarch
¼   cup cold water
1   tablespoon butter
Dash of salt

Peel and slice apples and place them into a 2-quart pot.
Add water and white sugar. Cover and cook until tender.
    In a 1-quart pot melt butter and stir in brown sugar to
carmelize. The sugar forms syrup, and the butter
separates and appears like a stream of oil. Turn off heat
but continue to stir a bit. Let cool some.

Pour about 2 cups of juice off the apples into the caramel pot. Stir until all is blended and forms a caramel apple juice.

For the sauce, combine cornstarch and water. Stir in about ½ cup of warm juice from pot to neutralize the temperature of the starch juice. Add this mixture to the caramel juice, stirring constantly over low heat until the juice thickens and begins to shine as it boils to a thick butterscotch sauce. When this happens, the sauce is done. Add dash of salt and tablespoon of butter and stir.

Rhubarb Custard Pie

Serves 6 to 8.

4   cups rhubarb
1   egg, slightly beaten
1   cup sugar
3   tablespoons flour
½   cup water
1   tablespoon butter
piecrust, purchased or made as for apple pie (page 161) but with half the ingredients

Prepare 9-inch pie shell, unbaked. Cut rhubarb into ½-inch pieces. Mix all ingredients except rhubarb. Place rhubarb into shell and pour mixture over it. During baking, may press rhubarb down into juice with back of spoon to keep fruit moist.

Bake at 375° for 60 minutes or until crust is golden and fruit is bubbly around sides and center.

Butter Crumb Cake (Like Hough Bakery's!)

At our three o-clock coffee breaks, we often enjoyed Hough's butter crumb cake along with good conversations. This recipe from Sister Mary Ann Cirino is based on one handed down by Sister Mary St. Edward.

Serves 6 to 8.

1½ cups of flour
½   cup sugar
2   teaspoons baking power
½   teaspoon salt
2/3 cup milk
3   tablespoons melted butter
2   teaspoons vanilla or almond flavoring
1   egg

Topping:
2   tablespoons butter
½   cup flour
¼   cup breadcrumbs
½   teaspoon cinnamon
¼   cup finely chopped walnuts (optional)

Sift together flour, sugar, baking powder, and salt. Beat egg and milk and then add butter and vanilla. Mix this with dry ingredients. Pour mixture into a greased and floured 9 x 9-inch pan.

For the topping, mix together all the ingredients until they have a crumbly texture. Sprinkle the crumb topping over the mixture in the pan. Bake at 425° for 20 to 25 minutes.

Baked Alaska Ice Cream Dessert

4 servings.

1½ quarts of your favorite ice cream (will not need all)
12 ladyfingers (or 3 x 2-inch slices of sponge or pound cake)
4   egg whites at room temperature
¼   teaspoon salt
1/8 teaspoon cream of tartar
2/3 cup sugar
½   teaspoon of vanilla extract (optional)

Start about an hour before serving. Preheat oven to 500° about 20 minutes before baking.

Scoop four 4 or 5 ounce portions of ice cream and place in freezer. You may use a #8 scoop or a 4-ounce measure. (*Option:* You may scoop ice cream onto the cake at this point and freeze the whole portion.)

About an hour before serving, arrange three whole ladyfingers or cake slices evenly spaced on a 13-inch baking pizza stone or other baking pan.

For the meringue, in a mixer place egg whites, cream of tartar, salt, and vanilla flavoring and beat with whip attachment on medium speed, adding sugar 2 tablespoons at a time until soft peaks form. Then beat on high speed until stiff peaks form.

Using a spatula or butter knife quickly spread the meringue over the ice cream scoops, sealing at base of ice cream onto the cake. Swirl the meringue into little points for an attractive look. Bake 3 to 4 minutes until golden at edges. Watch carefully! Remove and serve immediately. (Before it is springtime in Alaska!)

Lamb Cake

(Created with Griswold cast iron mold)
To make a lamb cake you need to set aside a few hours
and have lots of patience. This is a delicate process, but a
rewarding sense of accomplishment awaits you when it's
completed. The frosted Easter lamb displayed on a platter
on your dining room table on Easter Day is worth all the
effort. The lamb is a symbol of what Easter is all about,
therefore a custom that deserves to be kept!

½ cup shortening
1½ cup sugar
3   eggs
1   cup milk
2½ cup flour
4   teaspoons baking powder
½   teaspoon salt
1   teaspoon vanilla
Frosting
¼ pound shredded coconut
Green food coloring (optional)

Sift together dry ingredients. Add vanilla to the milk.
Cream shortening well, adding sugar gradually. Add
well-beaten yolks and cream again. Alternately add dry
ingredients and milk. Lastly fold in beaten egg whites.
Bake for 25 minutes, and then turn over and bake for 20
minutes. Placing a toothpick in each ear will support that
part of cake. Cupcakes can be made from any excess
batter.
    The cake batter can be made from any cake mix or
from a recipe that provides a firm cake (like pound cake).

After baking, let cool completely before frosting with favorite frosting. Cover lamb with coconut. If you wish, color some coconut green to make grass around the lamb.

Paradise Pudding

This favorite recipe was a way to use up leftover cake.

Serves 12.

1   6-ounce package red jello
1   8-ounce can of fruit cocktail
1   8-ounce carton frozen Cool Whip (defrosted)
2   cups boiling hot water (to dissolve jello)
Cold water (to add to drained fruit juice)
1½ cups pound cake, cubed
Walnuts, crushed (optional)

Drain fruit cocktail and save juice. Place fruit in 9 x 13-inch baking dish. Scatter cake cubes over the fruit. In a 2-quart mixing bowl, add 2 cups boiling water to dry jello. Stir to dissolve completely.

Add cold water to fruit juice to make 2 cups. Pour cold liquid into jello mixture. Chill this until syrup, then pour it over the ingredients in the baking dish. Fold in Cool Whip, allowing it to stream through and form clouds. Let set.

Cut dish of jello into squares and serve on a platter or scoop into parfait glasses. Garnish with crushed walnuts on top.

Whipped Cream Icing

½   cup margarine
½   cup Crisco
1   cup powdered sugar
1   teaspoon vanilla
¾   cup milk

Boil milk on low heat. Don't skim off top. Let cool. Beat margarine, Crisco, and vanilla together. Add powdered sugar slowly to creamed mix. Slowly add cooled milk and continue beating. Return mixture to pot on stove. Gradually turn to high and beat about 7 minutes.

Notre Dame Style Apple Pie

It is fitting to conclude my book with the recipe for the apple pie served at the Notre Dame barbeques. This pie was made from Notre Dame orchard apples. For many years it was prepared by the hands of Sisters young and old and enjoyed by thousands of friends and relatives of Notre Dame. In their pie making, Sisters truly conveyed their community mission to spread God's goodness to all.

Serves 12 (two 9 ½-inch pies).

Piecrust:
3   cups all-purpose flour
1   teaspoon salt
1   cup pork lard
5-6 tablespoons ice cold water

Filling:
½ teaspoon tapioca
12 (8 cups) apples, three varieties, ½ sweet and ½ tart (I
suggest Mcintosh, Jonathan, and a tart apple like
Granny Smith)
1 cup sugar
½ teaspoon cinnamon

Topping:
Same as for piecrust but without water

Advice for beginners: Your goal is golden, flaky
pastry that cuts easily. Do not over handle because
hot hands melt shortening, which should be chilled.
Avoid adding too much flour or too much water
when rolling the dough.

Add salt to flour. Work flour into fat with a circular
motion lightly so as not to melt the fat, or use a pastry
blender. Add cold water to the dough one tablespoon at a
time. The dough should be moist but not pasty. Toss it
gently as you mix with fingers.

On a lightly floured table, divide the dough into two
parts for two pies. Gently form each part into a ball and
then flatten it. Sprinkle dough lightly with flour. With a
floured rolling pin, roll dough forward and backward and
then left to right. With floured fingers, pick up the dough,
dust the table with flour again, turn over the dough and
roll it again. Turn and roll the dough two or three times
until you have a circle 2 inches larger than the pie pan.

Carefully fold the pie circle in half, and place the folded side in the center of a 9-inch pie dish. Open the dough and fit it loosely into dish. Pat it gently into place leaving no air pockets between crust and pan. Press the edges of the dough against the rim of the pie pan. Then sprinkle tapioca over the shell to thicken the apple juice that develops as apples bake.

Mix the cinnamon and sugar in a quart-size bowl. Peel and chop the apples to gravel size by hand or in a Cuisinart processor. (Chopped apples are more evenly cooked and flavored.) Fill each shell with some of the apples, pushing them to the edge and filling in all spaces. Sprinkle the sugar mixture over the apples. Add another layer of apples so that it forms a mound. The center will sink during baking.

With a butter knife trim excess dough extending over the edge. Using your right index finger and thumb, pinch along the edge of the dough and twist inward toward the center of the pie, working counterclockwise.

Mix the topping ingredients. Measure out a cup or a good handful of this dry mix and sprinkle it generously over the whole pie all the way to the edges. This dough prevents the apples from being singed.

Place pies on baking sheet because juice will bubble over. Place them side by side in the middle of the oven or position them so that one is not directly over the other. Bake for approximately 1 hour in preheated 400° oven. As the pies cook, there will be bubbling around the edges and the mound of apples will sink. Remove pies when time is up and crumb crust on top is golden.

Let pies sit on drip tray to cool. With a wet cloth wipe excess syrup from bottom of pie dish. Cool completely before serving. Delicious with vanilla ice cream!

Preparing Pies for the Barbeques

The oldest and youngest Sisters peeled and cut all the apples during the weeks preceding the barbeque weekends. Once this was done, cook Sisters chopped the apples to just the right size according to Sister Dorotheus's instruction. Usually a trusted specialist like Sister Mary Thaddea was allowed to do this. And only Sister Dorotheus and two or three other Sisters like Sisters Eileen Reardon, Theresa Gebura, and Stefana Osredkar were skilled enough to roll the pie shells. The rest of us mixed dough or filled pies.

A huge batch of pies was made in the early summer and frozen. Then in the week before the September barbeque, the last big bake off took place. Pies were everywhere that week and then frozen! Barbeque day was spent reheating them.

EPILOG

I hope you have enjoyed the glimpse inside the cloister.
The early years at the convent on a hill in Geauga County
were the foundation of my culinary career. It was there
that I learned all the basics of cooking, religious life in
community, and most of all I began the close walk with
Jesus that endures today.

The culinary traditions of this wonderful community
of Notre Dame were a fascinating discovery for a small
town girl from Warren, Ohio, who rarely set foot in her
mother's kitchen!

My sister Bonnie's favorite song was "All Good
Gifts" from the musical *Godspell.* My companions at the
outset of my journey in foodservice—the cook Sisters
and other Sisters too—instructed and encouraged me.
They were truly God's gifts.

For each of them and for all his good gifts,

I thank the Lord!

Appendix

HELPFUL TABLES

Equivalent Measures

1 tablespoon	3 teaspoons
¼ cup	4 tablespoons
½ cup	8 tablespoons
1 cup	16 tablespoons
1 pint	2 cups
1 quart	4 cups
1 gallon	4 quarts
1 pound	16 ounces

Food Equivalents

Butter, 1 stick or ¼ pound	½ cup
Cheese, ¼ pound	1 cup shredded
Cottage cheese, 8 ounces	1 cup
All-purpose flour, 1 pound Cake flour	About 3 ½ cup About 4 cups
Onion, 1 large	¾ to 1 cup chopped
Rice, regular long grain	3 cups cooked
Sugar, 1 pound granulated Brown sugar, 1 pound Confectioner's sugar, 1 pound	2 ¼ to 2 ½ cups 2 ¼ cup packed 4 to 4½ cups

ABOUT THE AUTHOR

Mary Ann Quinn is a Dietetic Technician Registered (D.T.R.) and a member of the Academy of Nutrition and Dietetics. Currently she is Director of Nutrition Services Holly Hill Nursing Home and Assisted Living in Newbury, Ohio. She is in her tenth year of employment there and coordinates a staff of about twelve. Previously she worked in long term care at Villa Sancta Anna Home for the Aged in Beachwood, Ohio, until it closed. Before that, she worked at The Greens of Lyndhurst as it opened with Communicare of Ohio.

Formerly a Sister of Notre Dame for about twenty-five years, Mary Ann remains closely associated with them. She lives in Richmond Heights within walking distance of her church, Saint Paschal Baylon Parish in Highland Heights. There she has served on the Arts and Environment Committee and as a lector and Eucharistic minister.

In this book Mary Ann relates how meaningful the Eucharist is to her. Coincidentally, her parish is staffed by the Blessed Sacrament priests and brothers, whose charism is promoting the Eucharist. In addition, Saint Paschal Baylon, the patron saint of the parish, was a Franciscan friar who cooked for his community. He is famous for his mole sauce of culinary renown. Paschal also had a fondness for cats and is often portrayed in pictures with one at his feet. Mary Ann shares her house not only with Karen Mansi, who is a retired florist and grandmother of six, but with four cats. She has rescued several animals and entrusted them to the Animal Protective League.

When time permits, Mary Ann enjoys visiting family and friends, pursuing her genealogy, hiking, swimming, reading, and listening to good 50s and 60s music. Now besides being a D.T.R. Mary Ann is an author, who hopes readers enjoy her book.

Saint Paschal Baylon, OFM
1540-1592
Feast Day - May 17

Made in the USA
Middletown, DE
20 September 2016